SHAKESPEARE'S SONNETS:

THEIR RELATION TO HIS LIFE

AMS PRESS

NEW YORK

SHAKESPEARE'S SONNETS:

THEIR RELATION TO HIS LIFE

BY

BARBARA A. MACKENZIE

M.A., D.Litt. (Cape Town) ; B.Litt. (Oxon) ;
Senior Lecturer at the University College of the O.F.S.

Your monument shall be my gentle verse,
Which eyes not yet created shall o'er-read
(SHAKESPEARE TO SOUTHAMPTON)

MASKEW MILLER LIMITED
CAPE TOWN
1946

Library of Congress Cataloging in Publication Data

Mackenzie, Barbara Alida.
    Shakespeare's sonnets.

    Reprint of the 1946 ed. published by M. Miller,
Cape Town.
    Bibliography: p.
    Includes index.
    1. Shakespeare, William, 1564-1616. Sonnets.
2. Shakespeare, William, 1564-1616—Friends and
associates. 3. Sonnets, English—History and criti-
cism. 4. Dramatists, English—Early modern, 1500-1700
—Biography. I. Title.
PR2848.M24   1978   821'.3   78-6965
ISBN 0-404-04135-3

First AMS edition published in 1978.

Reprinted from the edition of 1946, Capetown. [Trim
size and text area of the original have been slightly
reduced in this edition. Original trim size: 13.3 x 20.2 cm;
text area: 10.1 x 15.1 cm.]

MANUFACTURED
IN THE UNITED STATES OF AMERICA

CONTENTS

PREFACE

This monograph on Shakespeare's Sonnets is the outcome of many years' work on and consideration of the sonnets and of whatever evidence we possess concerning Shakespeare's life and the lives of those connected with him.

As regards the re-arrangement, the grouping and the interpretation of the sonnets, I have relied solely on the results of my own investigations. I have in the course of my work sedulously and deliberately avoided consulting the conclusions reached by other recent critics in the field, as I wished to evade the insidious danger of unconscious copying and to feel that my results, whatever their value or interest, were genuinely my own, free from outside influence. It was only after I had completed my investigations and embodied them in this monograph that I turned to consult the work of the leading critics in the fields of Shakespearian sonnet research, such as Tucker Brooke and the late J. A. Fort. I had read brief reviews of their books, but nothing more. Any resemblances, therefore, that may be found between my conclusions and theirs are the result of pure coincidence.

My obligations, however, to the work of earlier scholars such as the late Sir Edmund Chambers, Dr. Leslie Hotson, Dr. G. B. Harrison, Mrs. Stopes, and the late Sir Sidney Lee are considerable, and I have endeavoured to acknowledge my debts at the appropriate place in the text.

I should like to express my grateful thanks to the Librarian and his staff at the University of Cape Town. The facilities granted me there have been of the greatest value in the writing of this study.

For the sake of securing uniformity with the sonnets, the spelling in all quotations from documents, literary works, etc., belonging to the Elizabethan period has been modernized.

BARBARA A. MACKENZIE.

University College of the Orange Free State,
Bloemfontein.

INTRODUCTION

The full story that lies behind the sonnets of Shakespeare will in all probability never be known. Fragmentary facts about the poet and his concerns have drifted down from the Elizabethan age, and have been assiduously collected by the patient industry of scholars and researchers. Can these facts be related to the tale told by the sonnets ? Does this famous sequence give exciting life and substance to a dry entry in a register, or is it to be regarded only as a bloodless literary exercise ? It would be delightful to be in a position to prove by conclusive documentary evidence a relationship between the sonnets and the author's life, but such a miracle is not likely to occur. Other methods, however, are still open to the researcher to-day. Let us remember that three-and-a-half centuries separate us from those crucial years in Shakespeare's life when he was writing the sonnets, and that during this period there have been great changes in human life and ways of thinking. We live now in a highly mechanized age, to which precision and proof are of major importance. Imagination has fallen from the proud eminence she enjoyed in Elizabethan times, and become a creature of doubtful reputation. Yet she still has the power to guide us to the truth when factual resources fail. How without sympathetic imagination are we to understand that most emotional, most impressionable age ? Where are the tangible facts to prove the undoubted effects of great political issues or of dynamic personalities on the hearts of men at that time ? The imagination must play her part here, controlled indeed by common-sense.

The purpose of this study is to work from the solid foundation of the known facts or reasonable deductions about Shakespeare, his environment, and those personages with whom he came in contact during the probable period of sonnet-writing. Then is offered a conjectural, imaginative reconstruction of the effect that these incidents and people had upon the poet, and the sonnets are considered as giving voice to the poet's emotions at the time. In this way an attempt has been made to relate the sonnets in an intelligible manner to the personal experiences of Shakespeare.

The general conclusions I have reached in the course of this investigation are these.

I have taken the simple view that all the sonnets were written by Shakespeare. Many arguments have been set forth against the assumption of a single authorship of the sonnets, but they are all based on internal evidence, and their foundation seems shaky, to say the least. To assume that a particular sonnet is not by Shakespeare because it betrays a neurotic outlook is to say that Shakespeare was incapable of feeling the strain of nervous tension—an unlikely supposition and one which so cautious a scholar as Chambers contradicts. Sonnets, again, which reflect the style of authors such as Chapman, may be by a hand other than Shakespeare's, but they may equally well be by Shakespeare, the myriad-minded,

Desiring this man's art and that man's scope,

when in a fit of self-distrust he was imitating, or when he was merely under the passing influence of, some fashionable writer. G. B. Harrison (*Shakespeare at Work*, p. 307, note to passage on p. 8) remarks that a young writer's style is often imitative of that of more practised writers, and that it is unwise to build theories of other hands on the evidence of style in early work. Unevenness in the quality of the sonnets may be traced to the fact that they were written over a period of years. Finally, a sonnet that leaves an impression of triviality or weakness in style may well have been composed by Shakespeare himself under the stress of intense and immediate emotion, when the critical faculties were overwhelmed by the power of some intense personal feeling. It is enough to think of Keats when the shadow of Fanny Brawne fell upon his work, to realize what may happen under such conditions. All the objectors to the theory of sole Shakespearian authorship have assumed that the poet could write only good and fully characteristic lines even in 1592 or 1593, at the beginning of his career—an attitude that is too reminiscent of the idolatry of the Romantic age. Poor lines and imitative lines are to be found in the signed poems, for that matter. To split up the sonnets among several writers is a procedure more rash than to assume they are what they pretend to be—Shakespeare's sonnets. And, as far as we know, Shakespeare never denied that he was the sole author, nor did anyone else lay claim to any share in the writing of the sonnets.

I do not think that the sonnets as a whole form a mere literary exercise. The earliest in the sequence, as we now have it, may well have been written to order and with an eye to publication. But soon the human element creeps in. As the formal acquaintance between patron and poet warms first to friendship and then to noble love, the idea of publication is given up, and the sonnets take the form of spontaneous and personal revelations too intimate for the public eye. I believe that the sonnets are autobiographical and that after the first few they allude directly to personal experiences or to definite events touching Shakespeare's life. They are not fanciful or divorced from reality, but refer to matters familiar to both writer and recipient : hence the obscurity to us of many of the references. Shakespeare may employ some conventional phraseology or turn of thought, but this does not impair the authentic note of personal reaction in the sonnets. They were written impulsively, on the spur of the moment, almost as if they were letters addressed to the friend. Perhaps they were.

I see no reason for doubting that the sonnets were addressed to two people, and to two people only—Southampton and the enigmatic " Dark Lady ". Changes in the tone of the address and in the attitude of mind revealed in different sonnets may be quite simply explained by the gradual growth in affection for the friend, by the effect of the impact of various external events on the poet, and so forth. By correlating the known events in the lives of Shakespeare and of Southampton with those adumbrated in the sonnets, I have found nothing that renders Southampton impossible as the male recipient, and everything that points to him as the " fair friend ".

As regards the date of composition of the sonnets, this investigation has led me to the conclusion that the sequence was begun early in 1592 (or late in 1591) and brought to an end during the first half of 1596.

The sonnets as printed in the Quarto of 1609 are not in their original order, but the main outlines of the story are even there fairly clear. Some re-shuffling of the order is necessary, but it is not of a radical nature. Style, substance and sentiment have all to be taken into account whenever a change in the traditional order appears necessary. When this re-grouping is considered in the light of the known facts about poet and patron, certain interesting features emerge. The story told by the sonnets takes on a coherent shape, and a distinct development in the relationship between poet and friend can be traced.

The problem of the rival poet has produced several rivals to contend for the honour of having excited in Shakespeare a passion of fear and jealousy. What emerges from this study is that the sonnets suggest we have to deal not with one rival poet but with three rival writers, though one (whom I identify as Barnabe Barnes) is of major importance because of the number of sonnets directed at him and his works.

Various other elements present themselves for consideration, and notably the incident alluded to in Sonnet 112. This one I consider to be of the greatest interest and value in throwing light on the history of the sonnets, yet its significance has been completely overlooked by commentators. It is possible to date this sonnet with precision, and we gain from it an insight into Shakespeare's nature, while its position in the sequence throws light on the confused order in which we have the sonnets to-day.

Attempts to identify the " Dark Lady " have hitherto not met with much success, and I have little fresh light to throw on this problem. There are at best some intriguing and suggestive clues which I have noted, and they may lead anywhere or nowhere. But this problem of the " Dark Lady " is perhaps of minor importance. Shakespeare himself seems to have regarded her as insignificant compared with his " best of dearest ".

As for Mr. W. H., I cannot better the suggestion that he was Mr. (or Sir) William Harvey, and that he was merely the instrument through whom the sonnets achieved initial publication. Yet I have added a possible explanation why *he* was the one to be so officious in the business of getting the sonnets printed without, apparently, the knowledge or approval of either Shakespeare or Southampton.

In conclusion, I have seen no trace of anything abnormal or sensational in the relation between poet and patron. We have to deal simply with a passionate friendship, unsullied by any taint of perversion. It ran its course over rough and smooth, and it ended—leaving Shakespeare the loser as a man, the gainer in infinite measure as a dramatist.

SHAKESPEARE'S SONNETS

THE YOUNG SOUTHAMPTON AND THE MARRIAGE PROBLEM

In 1565 the second Earl of Southampton was married to Mary Browne, then aged thirteen. The Earl was wealthy and lived in a style of lavish magnificence, but it must have been a relief to his lovely and still youthful wife when he died in 1581, for he was a tyrant in his behaviour towards her. He left as his heir his son Henry Wriothesley, who had been born on 6th October, 1573. The young third Earl of Southampton was sent in 1585 to St. John's College, Cambridge, where he developed his love of literature, and graduated with the degree of M.A. in 1589.

When the young nobleman came to London shortly after this, he was a notable figure. He possessed wealth and a lofty title, he had cultured tastes, and he was strikingly handsome. His early portraits confirm his reputation for beauty. They show him slender and graceful in figure. His long fair hair is curled back over the top of his head and falls, thick and waved, over the shoulder and across the breast. The beautiful intelligent eyes are clear and blue, with a thoughtful, direct and faintly smiling glance. The features are handsome and boyish, but the full lower lip gives a touch of petulance to the expression.

As Southampton was the only male representative of his line, it was obviously urgent that he should marry soon. But to the dismay of his relatives the Earl declined to do anything of the sort. Frantic efforts were made to induce him to see reason. In vain Lord Burleigh offered his granddaughter, the Lady Elizabeth Vere. In 1590 Sir Thomas Stanhope was thought to be trying to foist his daughter on the Elizabethan Adonis, and in self-defence he immediately wrote a letter to Burleigh, denying he had entertained any such idea.

Irritation was growing on all sides. The stately Burleigh was affronted by the Earl's unwillingness to accept the Lady Elizabeth ; the Countess was distracted by her son's attitude, and tearfully implored the advice of her friends ; the situation became a topic of gossip at Court. At last the badgered young Earl, taking matters into his own hands, fled across the Channel to Dieppe to escape commands and exhortations. From there he wrote a letter to the Earl of Essex, begging that dashing and picturesque hero, who was at the time engaged on military operations on the Continent, to give him a refuge by accepting him as a volunteer for foreign service. Essex would hardly have cared to embroil himself with powerful personages by championing the runaway, and the fugitive, sulky and still obstinate, was dragged back to London early in 1591.

II.

MEETING OF SHAKESPEARE AND SOUTHAMPTON

The family were far from abandoning the marriage campaign, and a new plan caused the paths of Shakespeare and Southampton to cross. We can only guess how the Southamptons originally came in contact with the still obscure actor and play-writer. It seems likely that one of the heroes of '88, Mr. William Harvey, who may already have been a friend of the family, suggested the plan that Shakespeare should be approached to write a sequence of sonnets. In the spring of 1591 Sir Philip Sidney's *Astrophel and Stella* had been posthumously published, and was being eagerly read by everyone. Sonnet sequences suddenly became the fashion. Let the book-loving young nobleman be addressed through this medium and implored to select a bride : he who was deaf to a great statesman and to an affectionate mother might listen to a poet. Such may have been Harvey's advice, and the explanation would satisfactorily account for his later title of " begetter " of the sonnets.

Why was Shakespeare chosen for the task ? What connection had he with the Southampton family ? There is one frail link which has possibilities not to be overlooked, and that is the suggestion that Shakespeare had already become acquainted with Southampton's Italian tutor John Florio. On 30th April, 1591, Florio's *Second Fruits* was entered in the Stationers' Register, and to the work was prefixed a sonnet entitled *Phaethon to his Friend Florio*, and beginning :

Sweet friend, whose name agrees with thy increase,
How fit a rival art thou of the Spring !

It was suggested by W. Minto (*Characteristics of English Poets*, 1885) that Shakespeare may have been the author of this sonnet. Chambers (*William Shakespeare : Facts and Problems*, Vol. I., p. 555) thinks that of all the anonymous poems ascribed to Shakespeare it alone is deserving of consideration ; and, though he is not convinced that Shakespeare wrote it, he says that the sonnet " has merit ". If Shakespeare actually knew Florio in the spring of 1591, and had proved to him his skill as a sonnet-writer, it is easy to understand that the Southampton family should decide to approach him with their poetic-matrimonial commission.

At this stage another problem makes its appearance : at what date did Shakespeare begin to write sonnets addressed to Southampton ? The almost certain date of one sonnet (112), which has so far been missed by critics, is of considerable importance as a guide. This sonnet belongs to the end of 1592, and the tone of it points to an already marked degree of intimacy between patron and poet. J. A. Fort (*A Time Scheme for Shakespeare's Sonnets*) has calculated that the first meeting took place during the spring, but Sonnet 112 puts back Fort's date, 1593, to 1592. It is not impossible, however, that Shakespeare may have begun his sequence as early as the late winter of 1591–2, judging by some internal indications which will be discussed in due course.

III.

THE SONNETS BEGUN

Possibly, then, in the winter of 1591–2, but perhaps more probably in the early spring of 1592, Shakespeare met Southampton for the first time, and was dazzled and enchanted by the handsome youth. The poet has often been accused of snobbish inclinations, but neither Southampton's " proud titles " nor his wealth interested him. Shakespeare had received his commission to address the youth in strains as fervent and as exquisitely fashioned as his muse could devise, and he chose to base his passionate plea for marriage solely on the young Earl's obligation to perpetuate his beauty.

The sonnets in the beginning were not spontaneous effusions but a literary task commissioned by wealthy and distinguished patrons, and there must have been some idea of having them published. But, as time went on, the original purpose was lost sight of ; the marriage theme was dropped, along with the impersonal attitude of the poet, as he began to find his affections more and more involved, until the sonnets developed into a medium through which Shakespeare, addressing his friend, recorded the joys and torments of his heart during nearly five of the most emotional and significant years of his life.

It may be well at this point to summarize my view of the story embodied in the sonnets and of the order in which I take them to have been written.

CHRONOLOGICAL TABLE OF EVENTS RECORDED IN THE SONNETS.

(* *An asterisk indicates a new interpretation.*)

SECTION IV. (late 1591 or early 1592) :
Sonnets 1–7, 9, 11, 8, 12, 14, 10, 13, 17, 15, 16, 126.

Shakespeare adjures Southampton to marry in order to perpetuate his beauty. Acquaintance ripens to friendship.

SECTION V. (early 1592) :
Sonnets 18, 19, 63, 65, 99, 106, 67, 68.

Shakespeare confidently promises to immortalize the friend's beauty by means of his verse. Marriage theme discarded.

SECTION VI. (early 1592) :
Sonnets 20, 22, 62, 24, 53, 54, 59, 60, 64, 30, 31, 55, 81.

The friendship develops into a deep affection.

SECTION VII. (summer and autumn, 1592) :
Sonnets 66, 77, 27, 28, 43.

London theatres closed. Shakespeare goes on tour with his company. The first absence. Shakespeare mourns the separation.

SECTION VIII. (autumn, 1592) :
Sonnets 44, 45, 46, 47, 39, 23.

*Southampton leaves London to attend Queen Elizabeth on one of her progresses. Shakespeare returns to London and, Southampton being still absent, writes *Venus and Adonis*.

SECTION IX. (autumn, 1592) :
Sonnets 71, 72, 111, 112, 29, 37.

*Greene's attack on Shakespeare published by Chettle. Shakespeare bewails his sense of humiliation, and loses confidence in his poetic powers.

SECTION X. (1592 ?):
    Sonnets 153, 154, 127, 132, 128, 130, 131, 135, 136, 143, 139, 140, 145, 151, 129, 146, 147, 141, 148, 150, 137, 138, 142, 149, 152.

Interlude : the " Dark Lady " wooed and won by Shakespeare. He becomes a prey to jealousy and self-contempt.

SECTION XI. (spring, 1593):
    Sonnets 50, 51, 113, 114.

London theatres again closed. Shakespeare in depressed mood goes on tour. The second absence. *Venus and Adonis* published.

SECTION XII. (May, 1593):
    Sonnet 25.

*Southampton disappointed in his hopes of receiving the Order of the Garter. Shakespeare consoles him.

SECTION XIII. (May, 1593 ?):
    Sonnets 48, 61, 91, 92, 93, 49.

Shakespeare, absent, hears rumours that Southampton is bestowing his patronage elsewhere, and expresses his anxiety.

SECTION XIV. (June, 1593 ?):
    Sonnets 21, 78, 79, 80, 83, 85, 86.

Barnes publishes *Parthenophil and Parthenope* with a dedication to Southampton. Shakespeare voices his fear and jealousy, and criticizes Barnes' artificial style.

SECTION XV. (late 1593):
    Sonnets 144, 133, 134, 33, 34, 35, 40, 41, 42.

Interlude : in Shakespeare's absence Southampton woos and wins the " Dark Lady." Shakespeare discovers this (on his return ?) and finally sacrifices love to friendship.

SECTION XVI. (early 1594):
    Sonnets 107, 115, 116, 122, 123, 124, 125, 32.

Shakespeare celebrates the renewal of friendship after a stormy experience, and writes *The Rape of Lucrece*.

SECTION XVII. (May, 1594):
    Sonnets 26, 38, 73, 74.

The Rape of Lucrece published. Shakespeare replies to Southampton's acknowledgments of the dedication, but gives vent to melancholy thoughts.

SECTION XVIII. (spring and summer, 1594):
    Sonnets 98, 56, 97, 52, 75.

Shakespeare again on tour. The third absence. Some mournful reflections on the separation.

SECTION XIX. (1594):
    Sonnets 76, 108.

*Nash's *Unfortunate Traveller* published with a dedication to Southampton. Shakespeare, jealous, attacks the novelty of the production.

SECTION XX. (autumn, 1594):
  Sonnets 36, 88.

Willobie His Avisa published. Shakespeare fears an allusion to the " Dark Lady " episode, expresses his anxiety, and offers to end the friendship with Southampton to protect the latter.

SECTION XXI. (early 1595):
  Sonnets 69, 70.

*Southampton assists the Danvers brothers to escape after the murder of Long. Shakespeare replies to the subsequent scandal attached to Southampton.

SECTION XXII. (early 1595):
  Sonnets 104, 105.

Shakespeare celebrates the third anniversary of the friendship and probably writes *Romeo and Juliet* for Southampton.

SECTION XXIII. (spring, 1595):
  Sonnets 100, 101, 102, 103.

Shakespeare fails to present the annual poem, and apologizes for his silence.

SECTION XXIV. (September, 1595):
  Sonnets 84, 82.

*Markham's *Sir Richard Grinvile* published with a dedication to Southampton. Shakespeare criticizes the vulgarity of the dedication and rebukes Southampton.

SECTION XXV. (October, 1595):
  Sonnets 95, 96, 94.

*Southampton in love with Elizabeth Vernon. Shakespeare warns Southampton of scandalous rumours, and composes *A Lover's Complaint.*

SECTION XXVI. (late 1595):
  Sonnets 57, 58.

Shakespeare makes abject apology to the angry Southampton for his interference.

SECTION XXVII. (early 1596):
  Sonnets 109, 110, 117, 118, 119, 120.

*Shakespeare, having written *A Midsummer-Night's Dream* for another patron, and having included a parody of *Romeo and Juliet*, makes further abject apologies to the furious Southampton.

SECTION XXVIII. (early summer, 1596):
  Sonnets 121, 89, 90, 87.

*Shakespeare faces domestic and professional difficulties, as well as a vicious attack (by Gardiner ?) on his character. Shakespeare implores his friend's forgiveness in vain, and takes a final farewell of him.

IV.

THE MARRIAGE THEME

The sonnets in the first batch (1—7) faithfully observe the contract. The youth's spring-like beauty, dramatically posed against a menacing background of winter and old age to come, is celebrated, and the poet with many ingenious arguments adjures him to marry :

That thereby beauty's rose might never die.

(*Sonnet* 1.)

In the first sonnet, too, the youth is hailed as the *herald* of the spring ; in the second the ravages of *forty winters* are described ; in the fifth *hideous winter* is pictured :

Sap check'd with frost, and lusty leaves quite gone.

In the sixth the plea is :

Then let not winter's ragged hand deface
In thee thy summer, ere thou be distill'd.

These references to winter may be a mere literary convention, but they would gain added point if they coincided with the actual season when the poet launched his appeal, in which case the date of the first meeting would be the winter of 1591–2.

The subject of marriage is continued in Sonnets 9 and 11, but in Sonnet 8 a personal note is introduced for the first time. Shakespeare had become a little more intimate with the Earl. Perhaps he had been invited to an evening of music at his patron's house in Holborn. Shakespeare was undoubtedly an ardent lover of music, and, hearing a disparaging remark on the subject from Southampton, he expresses his surprise :

Music to hear, why hear'st thou music sadly ?

.   .   .   .

If the true concord of well-tunèd sounds
By unions married do offend thine ear,
They do but sweetly chide thee   .   .   .   .

and then goes on to turn this discovery to account in urging his plea for marriage.

The friendship progressed, and the poet began to drop the impersonal attitude he had sustained till now. In Sonnets 12 and 14 he speaks to the patron in the first person, and Sonnet 10 takes him a step further. Southampton had been *gracious and kind*, so the poet ventures a warmer and more intimate tone, concluding :

> Make thee another self for love of me,
> That beauty still may live in thine or thee.

At this point young Southampton defended his celibacy by protesting that he belonged to himself and had a right to dispose of himself when and as he thought fit. To this the poet replies in Sonnet 13. He boldly addresses his friend as *love* and *dear my love*, exhorting him to remember

> The barren rage of death's eternal cold.

Southampton, unmoved by his poet's arguments, but charmed by the " sug'red sweetness" of his verse, suggested that he might find sufficient immortality for his qualities through the medium of Shakespeare's poetry. Shakespeare hesitated.

> Who will believe my verse in time to come,
> If it were fill'd with your most high deserts ?

he asks in Sonnet 17. But he was flattered by the idea, while not forgetting his mission, and toyed with the possibility :

> But were some child of yours alive that time,
> You should live twice—in it and in my rhyme.

Sonnet 15 is a promise to carry out the new task of immortalizing the friend's youth and beauty in poetry. In Sonnet 16, however, uncertain whether his *pupil pen* and *barren rhyme* will prove equal to the occasion, the novice poet and dramatist still urges marriage as a *mightier way* and, harking back to the Earl's previous objection, assures him :

> To give away yourself keeps yourself still.

Here we may consider Sonnet 126, which seems to belong to this group by virtue of its tone and style. There is an air of intimacy about this sonnet, in which the friend is addressed as *my lovely boy.* The theme is that beauty passes. The sonnet, however, is irregular and incomplete : if it is intended as a sonnet, the couplet which should clinch the argument is missing. It would be amusing to imagine that Shakespeare had become as bored with the marriage theme as his refractory pupil had long been, and that this piece of verse was abandoned unfinished and in the rough when a newer and more exciting inspiration loomed up !

V.

IMMORTALITY THROUGH VERSE

The commissioned marriage theme was now dropped for good, and Shakespeare embarked on a more congenial business—that of immortalizing his friend's beauty in his verse. The earlier note of uncertainty disappears from the sonnets belonging to this period, and the poet is filled with a sense of splendid confidence. Sonnet 18 promises a triumph over death, and the boast :

> So long as men can breathe, or eyes can see,
> So long lives this, and this gives life to thee,

may refer to the sonnets (in which case the idea of publication was still present), or to the contemplated *Venus and Adonis,* perhaps already (1592) begun at the suggestion of Southampton.

I do not consider the theory that *Venus and Adonis* had been written before the poet met Southampton, and that Shakespeare had made the first advances by approaching him with the request that he should extend his patronage to the *first heir* of the poet's *invention,* a possible one. To begin with, the argument of Venus, directed at the unwilling Adonis :

> . . . . . . beauty breedeth beauty ;
> Thou wert begot,—to get it is thy duty,

is ridiculous in that setting, but is understandable if borrowed from the earlier sonnets to Southampton. Furthermore, Shakespeare seems to have written poems only by request and not on his own initiative. Only two poems besides the sonnets— *Venus and Adonis* and *The Rape of Lucrece*—are certainly from his pen, and two less certainly—*A Lover's Complaint* and *The*

Phoenix and Turtle. This suggests that he had little natural inclination for this form of poetic expression. Finally, the poet was a shy, retiring man ; he might write by request, but would hardly be the one to hawk his wares and importune patronage, like a Barnes or a Nash. A little later his feelings were to be deeply hurt by what he considered the Earl's easy acceptance of the offerings of outsiders who had no purpose but to *sell* and whose works had no real claim that they were inspired by persona devotion to the patron.

Sonnet 18 proudly claimed immortality for the poet's verse, and asserted its power to give eternal life to its subject. In Sonnet 19, however, the youth is ranked above the verse in importance, and the verse becomes a mere instrument :

> My love shall in my verse ever live young.

A touch of apprehension may be traced in the plea to Time :

> O carve not with thy hours my love's fair brow.

The reaction to over-confidence had come, and Shakespeare's apprehensions increase in Sonnet 63, in which he sadly admits that age must indeed overtake his *lover's life*, though the *sweet love's beauty* may be immortalized. Sonnet 65 continues the same theme with the hope

> That in black ink my love may still shine bright.

In a number of sonnets scattered through the sequence, the poet celebrates his friend's beauty, without reference to the destructive effects of Time or to the eternizing power of verse. These are not marked by any complexity in the emotion ; and, while their exact position in the original order is uncertain, their style suggests early composition, so that they may conveniently be considered at this point. According to Sonnet 99 the flowers have stolen from the loved one their beauty ; while Sonnet 106 proclaims that the friend is the fulfilment of the *prophecies* of beauty found in ancient books. In Sonnets 67 and 68 the friend's authentic beauty is celebrated in contrast with the *false painting,* the *bastard signs* of the present day.

So far has been traced the opening stage in the friendship, and the growing affection on the part of Shakespeare.

VI.

" MINE BE THY LOVE "

These gentle meditations on beauty were interrupted by a crisis, for in Sonnet 20, which has caused such unwarranted scandal and speculation, Shakespeare records with quivering intensity the friend's response to his affection. The affection was innocent and honourable, as the poet is at pains to point out in the sestet. Walter Thomson (*The Sonnets of Shakespeare and Southampton*, 1938) has shown that the term " passion " was commonly used at the time for " sonnet ", and further (op. cit., p. 24) that Shakespeare habitually employs the word in the general sense of deep (non-sexual) emotion or an outburst of feeling. There is not the slightest reason for reading into *the master-mistress of my passion* any hint of perversion.

In this sonnet the genuineness of Southampton's beauty and the integrity of his heart are celebrated, and thus the poem is linked in theme with Sonnets 67 and 68, alluded to above. It appears as if Shakespeare at this period had reason (or thought he had) to feel disgust at the arts of *false* women—a disgust that finds even more forcible expression in some of the " Dark Lady " sonnets which may have been written at the same time as Sonnet 20.

The reciprocated affection is further celebrated in Sonnet 22, with its intimate touches :

> Presume not on thy heart when mine is slain ;
> Thou gav'st me thine, not to give back again.

The spiritual identity of the friends is asserted in Sonnet 62, though there is an almost youthful pose of exaggeration in the poet's reference to himself :

> Beated and chopp'd with tann'd antiquity,

in contrast with the boyish beauty of Southampton.

In Sonnet 24 a new theme appears : not only is the loved one beautiful, but he possesses what the mere onlooker cannot perceive, a *heart*. Sonnet 53 exalts the *constant heart* above mere *external grace*, and Sonnet 54 proclaims that *beauty* seems more *beauteous* because of the added ornament of *truth.* In Sonnets 59 and 60 the friend becomes the eternal ideal of beauty and truth in a shifting world of change and decay, and the chosen subject of the poet's verse. This vision of change becomes overpowering for a moment in Sonnet 64, and the thought

> That Time will come and take my love away

brings home to Shakespeare how much he *fears to lose.* It is not clear whether this group of sonnets (59, 60, 64) preceded or followed 63 and 65, but the leading ideas are closely associated.

The melancholy strain is prolonged in Sonnets 30 and 31, in which memories telling of the work of Time—old woes, lost love, dead friends—are recalled ; but the comforting thought of the *dear friend* compensates for *all losses.* Perhaps at this point may be taken the bold, almost boastful assertions of Sonnets 55 and 81, with their proud promise of immortality through the medium of the poet's verse, with their confident proclamation that *this powerful rhyme* will outlive the *gilded monuments of princes*, and that

> Your monument shall be my gentle verse.
>
> (*Sonnet* 81.)

Incidentally, had Shakespeare, when he wrote Sonnets 55 and 81, the gorgeous monument of the Southamptons in mind, about the erection of which the second Earl had left such elaborate instructions in his will ?

My impression is that up to this point Shakespeare had been living in an exquisite dream-world, undisturbed by external events. Acquaintance with Southampton had ripened into friendship and then into love, and the love had been returned. It was Shakespeare's happiest time, when no cloud shadowed the love between the two men. The poet had not yet any reason to feel ashamed of his profession, or to doubt that his poetry was a glorious gift worthy of honour in the eyes of the greatest.

VII.

TRIALS OF AN ACTOR-DRAMATIST AND AN ABSENCE

At this point, I think, reality broke in. It seems quite possible that Shakespeare was at this period associated with the theatrical company known as Lord Strange's Men. These players, apparently, occupied the Rose Theatre and presented plays there from 19th February, 1592, producing Shakespeare's *Henry VI.* on 4th March and including it in their repertory thereafter.

Trouble, however, was brewing for the acting profession. Objections against the giving of plays on Sundays had been raised by the Puritan section in London, and the occurrence of an allegedly dangerous riot on 11th June, 1592, " about viij of the clock within the Borough of Southwark," near the theatres, was ascribed by them to the evil influence of play-giving on Sundays. The result of the complaint was that the Privy Council on 23rd June directed that " there be no plays used in any place near thereabouts ". In consequence the city theatres, including the Rose, were closed " until the feast of St. Michael " (Chambers, *Elizabethan Stage*, Vol. IV., pp. 310 *et sqq*).

This event woke Shakespeare from his happy dream. His livelihood was threatened, his profession insulted, he and his fellow-players victimized by the narrow-minded and prejudiced opinions of a powerful group. Far from adopting an attitude of remote and philosophic serenity, the actor-dramatist, I believe, wailed aloud his grief and resentment to his friend in Sonnet 66 :

> Tir'd with all these, for restful death I cry,—
> As, to behold desert a beggar born,
>
> . . . .
> And right perfection wrongfully disgrac'd
> And strength by limping sway disablèd,
> And art made tongue-tied by authority,
> And folly, doctor-like, controlling skill.

The sonnet breathes almost hysterical fury against tyrannous and gnorant oppression and the folly and injustice of the world. The poet, however, finds consolation in the thought of the friend's love (*cf.* Sonnets 30 and 31) :

> Tir'd with all these, from these would I be gone,
> Save that, to die, I leave my love alone.

Yet, great as was the poet's despair, there is no sign that he feels any stigma of disgrace attached to the dramatic profession, nor is there any shadow of doubt that the friend is both constant and sympathetic.

The unfortunate players, cast out of the theatres, had no alternative but to take to the road and go on tour in the provinces. Strange's Men may have gone to the Newington Butts Theatre, in the village of Newington, about a mile from London Bridge on the south bank and outside the city bounds. There is an undated order enjoining them to play there three days (it was rescinded within a short time), which may belong to this year or to 1591. Whichever date is correct (Chambers, *Elizabethan Stage*, Vol. IV., p. 311, thinks 1591 a " conceivable alternative " to 1592), an interesting possibility suggests itself as to what Shakespeare did at Newington besides acting. But this matter will be dealt with later.

At all events, Shakespeare was out of a London job, and Strange's Men, we know, were on a provincial tour by 13th July, apparently visiting Oxford on 6th October ; and they are recorded as having visited other places. Though there is nothing to prove it, Shakespeare may very well have been with the company that was producing his plays at this time—at least there is no indication that he was not, or that he was anywhere else.

The sonnets, too, indicate an absence from the friend, involving a toilsome and disagreeable journey. Perhaps Shakespeare presented Southampton with a blank book as a gift before leaving. Sonnet 77 records such a present, and the verse handles the subject of the ravages of Time, a theme much in the poet's mind at this period. (*Cf.* Sonnets 60, 63 above.) Shakespeare, as he did previously, rings changes on the ideas of Beauty, Time and the Mind in Sonnet 77. Perhaps a *glass* and a *dial* raised the number of the gifts to three and were intended to represent the poet's leading themes at the moment. It would at any rate have been a pretty idea.

Sonnets 27 and 28 bewail the poet's absence. His journeys, he laments, are toilsome, his days full of work, his nights made sleepless with longing for the far-off friend. Sonnet 28 reads like a doleful reply to a message of comfort and encouraging hopes that the return will be a happy occasion.

> How can I then return in happy plight,
> That am debarr'd the benefit of rest ?

complains the poet almost querulously ; and Sonnet 43 continues the lament over nights haunted by the face of the friend in dreams, and days made empty by his absence :

> All days are nights to see till I see thee,
> And nights bright days when dreams do show thee me.

VIII.

" THOU ART GONE " — *VENUS AND ADONIS*

Meanwhile, during the second half of 1592, Queen Elizabeth was indulging in one of her gorgeous progresses. She was at Oxford from 22nd to 28th September (Strange's Men are recorded as being there on 6th October), and Southampton was in her train. A poet, Mr. Philip Stringer, in an academic exercise published by the University Press on 10th October, praises the handsome nobles in her retinue, and above all for beauty and learning Southampton, " quo non formosior alter affuit "—for the poem was of course in Latin. (Stopes, *Life of Southampton*, p. 50 ; Lee, *Life of William Shakespeare*, p. 312.) Now the pair of sonnets, 44 and 45, may refer to a period when the friend himself had gone away.

> But ah, thought kills me that I am not thought,
> To leap large lengths of miles when thou art gone

is the cry in Sonnet 44, while Sonnet 45 continues to expatiate on the *death*, the *melancholy* of separation. It seems possible to refer the poet's wish to be brought

> From limits far remote, where thou dost stay,

of Sonnet 44 to Southampton's dutiful attendance on the Queen on this occasion.

One may imagine that the poet's pathetic wails over his sleepless nights or uneasy dreams haunted by shadows and images of the loved friend touched Southampton's heart. That he might not depend solely on the *soul's imaginary sight*, that much-painted young nobleman sent his despairing poet a portrait of himself to console him during their enforced absence from each other. This is acknowledged with rapturous gratitude in Sonnets 46 and 47, in which the poet employs the eye-and-heart conceit already used in Sonnet 24.

> Mine eye and heart are at a mortal war,
> How to divide the conquest of thy sight,

sings the poet in Sonnet 46 ; but the conclusion in Sonnet 47 is that the outcome of the conflict is a double blessing :

> So, either by thy picture or my love,
> Thyself away, art present still with me.

Perhaps during this separation Southampton sent an eager inquiry as to the progress of the poem that was to be dedicated to him and to immortalize his name. Shakespeare, already embarked on *Venus and Adonis*, sent Sonnet 39 in reply:

> O, how thy worth with manners may I sing,
> When thou art all the better part of me ?

(Who, by the way, was the worse part ? The " Dark Lady " ?) But the poet promises to employ the time profitably :

> Even for this let us divided live,
>
> .   .   .   .
>
> That by this separation I may give
> That due to thee, which thou deserv'st alone.
> O absence, what a torment wouldst thou prove,
> Were it not thy sour leisure gave sweet leave
> To entertain the time with thoughts of love,
>
> .   .   .   .
>
> And that thou teachest how to make one twain,
> By praising him here, who doth hence remain !

Incidentally, the references to *sour leisure, here* and *hence* suggest that Shakespeare, when he was writing this sonnet, had come back to London before the royal progress, with Southampton in its train, concluded on 9th October, and that he was officially idle, as Strange's Men had not yet re-opened their season in London. Actually, however, he was occupied in the creation of *Venus and Adonis*.

It was not long before the poem was completed ; and Shakespeare, in a state of intense excitement that made him feel physically weak, but still with full confidence in the power of his work's *eloquence,* presented the *first heir* of his *invention* to his beloved friend and patron. Afraid that in his nervous excitement words would fail him when he made the presentation, the agitated poet enclosed Sonnet 23, which reveals his state of mind and ends with the appeal :

> O learn to read what silent love hath writ,
> To hear with eyes belongs to love's fine wit.

Whose, by the way, was the *tongue that more hath more expressed* referred to in this sonnet ? Was this a jealous fling on the part of Shakespeare at the poor harmless academic poet of Oxford ? Or does it refer to John Clapham, who had dedicated his poem *Narcissus* to Southampton in 1591 ? (Stopes, *Life of Southampton,* p. 49, note.) That was surely a trifle, but it was Shakespeare's way to magnify trifling troubles and rebuffs, and to agonize loudly to his friend over matters that less sensitive souls might think deserved to be ignored. Shakespeare, however, was soon to meet a severer and more real trial than this perhaps imaginary one.

IX.

THE ATTACK BY GREENE

On 3rd September, 1592, died Robert Greene. While on his death-bed he had composed *Greenes Groats-worth of Wit* ; this was put into shape by Henry Chettle and appeared in the Stationers' Register on 20th September of the same year. This little work is famous for its ill-natured attack on certain dramatists, of whom Shakespeare alone is clearly indicated. In an abusive passage Greene calls Shakespeare an " upstart crow ", who " beautified " himself by stealing from the work of other dramatists, and who imagined he was " as well able to bombast out a blank verse as the best of you ". Greene goes on to label him " an absolute *Johannes fac totum* . . . in his own conceit the only Shake-scene in a country ". An assortment of insulting terms is hurled at Shakespeare and his like — " puppets ", " antics ", " apes ", " buckram gentlemen ", " peasants ", " rude grooms ", " painted monsters ". In fact, Shakespeare was publicly branded as a common fellow giving himself airs, a dishonest writer who stole his only good things from better authors, and in short a creature as conceited as he was despicable.

What did Shakespeare feel about this vicious and vulgar attack ? Those who delight to exalt him above the level of ordinary mankind, who see in him a " noble soul ", a " great mind " incapable of harbouring resentment against a miserable slanderer, and too loftily serene to pay the least attention to spiteful attacks of this kind, state or imply that he took no notice of Greene and his fulminations, feeling secure in his own greatness. Jusserand (*The English Novel in the Time of Shakespeare*, p. 165) states confidently : " Shakespeare, of course, did not answer." For a dramatist at the very threshold of his career to behave with such complacent self-assurance suggests an unmitigated prig of inhuman conceit. Was Shakespeare's such a repellent personality ? Harrison (*Shakespeare at Work*, p. 25) takes, however, the view that Shakespeare did protest against the cruel attack.

Very likely Shakespeare made no open protest : he was too shy, and he must have shrunk from joining in any public mud-slinging. But in private and to his *best of dearest* he gave vent to piercing cries of anguish and bitter humiliation in a number of sonnets, the true significance of which has been strangely overlooked by critics, though the key-word is there plain to read.

As we have seen, Shakespeare had just presented to Southampton, with anxious hopes and fears, his *Venus and Adonis*. Now, by a cruel blow, his fine confidence in his poetic powers was dashed. His work had been held up to public ridicule and shamefully insulted, his name had been jeered at, his pretensions of gentility mocked. His immediate reaction is seen in Sonnet 71. His thoughts fly to the idea of death as an escape from *this vile world*, fearful as death was to his sensitive mind. He wishes to be forgotten even by his friend :

> Do not so much as my poor name rehearse

(the name that Greene had made a jest of)

> Lest the wise world should look into your moan,
> And mock you with me after I am gone.

All very exaggerated, we may think, and unnecessarily morbid, but how much more human than the traditional picture of a calm disdain so popular among Shakespeare idolaters !

In Sonnet 72 the poet continues in the same vein of almost hysterical abjectness :

> . . . . . . dear love, forget me quite,
> For you in me can nothing worthy prove,
> Unless you would devise some virtuous lie.
>
> . . . .
> My name be buried where my body is,
> And live no more to shame nor me nor you.
> For I am shamed by that which I bring forth,
> And so should you, to love things nothing worth.

A *virtuous lie* to prove the poet's merit ? *Shamed ? Nothing worth ?* This is a new attitude for Shakespeare to adopt towards his work ! And then the curious harping on his name ! Shy uncertainty we have had before, but never this almost frantic sense of degradation that vibrates through these urgent lines. Greene had done his work well.

Shakespeare may have impulsively abandoned for the time all idea of publishing *Venus and Adonis*. It would be mocked and bring only discredit on its patron ! And at this point, too, he seems to have forgotten that the sonnets were supposed to be a mere literary exercise, intended for ultimate publication. Until now they had been suitable for the public eye, but henceforth their tenor was to be too intimate, too deeply emotional for strangers' eyes to *o'er-read.*

The poet was beside himself, but Southampton stood by him nobly. He tried to soothe and calm the distracted Shakespeare into a more reasonable frame of mind. This stage is indicated by Sonnet 111 :

> O, for my sake do you with fortune chide,
> The guilty goddess of my harmful deeds,
> That did not better for my life provide,
> Than public means, which public manners breeds.

Greene's pun on his name still rankles :

> Thence comes it that my name receives a brand.

The *willing patient* promises to abandon *bitterness* on one condition :

> Pity me, then, dear friend, and I assure ye,
> Even that your pity is enough to cure me.

It is in Sonnet 112 that the clues are plainest. Southampton did more than pity. Very likely he was among the " divers of worship " who approached Henry Chettle, the fat hack writer who had put the *Groats-worth of Wit* into shape for publication, and certainly Southampton could have " reported [Shakespeare's] uprightness of dealing, which argues his honesty, and his facetious grace in writing that approves his art." Who till now was familiar with the poet's writing, other than a couple of early plays, except Southampton and his friends ? Who more likely to have inspired that explanation and apology in Chettle's *Kind-Heart's Dream,* entered in the Stationers' Register on 8th December, 1592 ? Why was Chettle so pointedly polite to the novice dramatist in this apology, from which the above quotation is taken, and to no one else of the attacked, unless representations from an influential quarter had been made to him, and he had been duly chidden ? For Chettle humbly says, " I am as sorry as if the original fault had been my fault, because myself have seen his demeanour no less civil than he (is) excellent in the quality he professes."

Sonnet 112, I take it, was written after the apology had been made. Shakespeare seems to have received this olive branch with little graciousness. Only the friend's *love and pity* will fill the impression

> Which vulgar scandal stamp'd upon my brow.

And now Shakespeare repays the rankling pun of " Shake-scene " with a parallel pun—*o'er-green,* printed *ore-greene* in the Quarto. This curious verb occurs nowhere else in Shakespeare's work. Onions, in his *Shakespeare Glossary,* interprets it as " to cover (evil) with something pleasing ", without noticing the verbal implication in the word. Tucker, in his edition of the sonnets, finds it necessary to suggest that this peculiar word may be a misprint for " o'er-grain " (*op. cit.,* p. 188). But there is no need for such heroic measures. Shakespeare is simply implying that the friend can obliterate Greene's insult with his love and pity.

Both Greene's abuse and Chettle's subsequent apology are referred to in the lines :

> For what care I who calls me well or ill,
> So you o'er-green my bad, my good allow ?
> You are my all-the-world, and I must strive
> To know my shames and praises from your tongue.
>
> .　　.　　.　　.　　.　　.　　.
>
> In so profound abysm I throw all care
> Of others' voices, that my adder's sense
> To critic and to flatterer stoppèd are.

Is the last image an echo of Greene's " I have long with the deaf adder stopt mine ears . . . " ? (*Repentance*, in the *Groats-worth of Wit*.)

Sonnets 29 and 37 depict the last heavings of the stormy sea. The *disgrace*, the *outcast state* are still bewailed in Sonnet 29 with *bootless cries* ; the poet desires to possess whatever he most lacks :

> With what I must enjoy contented least,

but the thought of the friend compensates for all—the *leitmotif* of the moment :

> For thy sweet love remember'd such wealth brings,
> That then I scorn to change my state with kings.

(There is a ring of ominous prophecy in the last line.)

Sonnet 37 expresses the same idea :

> So I, made lame by fortune's dearest spite,
> Take all my comfort of thy worth and truth,
>
> .　　.　　.　　.　　.　　.　　.
>
> So then I am not lame, poor nor despis'd.

The Greene episode marks a turning point in the story told by the sonnets and provides a date of the highest value. Before the last months of 1592 the friendship between Shakespeare and Southampton had ripened into a close affection ; after that date their love gained in depth. Thanks to this attack by Greene, however, the sonnets had become unfit for publication ; their tone had developed into one too intimate for general perusal. Furthermore, Shakespeare's happy confidence in himself and his powers had received a severe blow : his low social status had

been brutally pointed out to him and his poetry had been stigma
tized as stolen goods. Perhaps many of his subsequent actions
may be traced to this experience. Finally, this affair gives us a
strange and valuable insight into the poet's innermost nature,
his personality, his reaction to external events. The man
Shakespeare comes alive.

It is for these reasons that I regard this group of sonnets as
of prime importance. The whole sequence may be considered as
pivoting on them—a pre-Greene and a post-Greene series. Also
they confirm the impression that the sonnets are inspired largely
by external facts ; their history does not lie entirely within.
Here is no myth, no dramatic creation, but humanity in the
living flesh.

X.

THE DARK LADY WOOED AND WON BY
THE POET

At this point it may be convenient to consider the problem
of the Dark Lady, or the Black Woman, as she has been less
respectfully called. Who she was, where, how or when Shakespeare met her, will perhaps remain in doubt for ever. The only
possible clue is afforded by the curious *Willobie His Avisa*, which
appeared in 1594 and which will be considered in detail later.
The story this book tells was very probably composed by an
imperfectly informed outsider—if indeed it actually refers to the
situation that arose in the lives of Shakespeare, another man and
this woman. The book was certainly libellous to some extent (as
the direction for its withdrawal in the Stationers' Register on
4th June, 1599, indicates), and so the writer would naturally wish
to cover up his traces partly but not wholly, or the point would
be lost. The vague " Cerne Dorset " reference may be a blind,
but the more definite fact that Avisa lived at the Inn of St. George
suggests interesting possibilities.

In 1591 or 1592—as has been noted earlier—Strange's Men
were directed by the Privy Council to leave the Rose Theatre
and transfer to the theatre of Newington Butts. This obscure
playhouse " stood at Newington, a village one mile from London
Bridge, divided from the Bankside by St. George's Fields, and
reachable by the road which continued Southwark High Street "

(Chambers, *Elizabethan Stage*, Vol. II., p. 404). Incidentally, it was " in the Windmill in St. George's Fields " that Shallow and Falstaff spent a merry night (*Henry IV., Part II.*, III., ii.), and the latter was greatly put out by the recollection. Why " Windmill," by the way ? Is this an echo of the " substantial " player's remark in Greene's *Groats-worth of Wit*, when he interrupted Roberto's " passion," that he was " reputed able at my proper cost to build a Windmill," so flourishing were his circumstances ? To return to the point, it is conceivable that there was actually a St. George's Inn in the vicinity of the Fields, from which it took its name, and of Newington ; and here Shakespeare, if he were associated with Strange's Men at this time, may well have met his Dark Lady, as Willobie hints. It is interesting to note that Russell Thorndike, in *A Wanderer with Shakespeare* (p. 40), mentions a George Inn in Southwark, still existing in a railway yard, which dates back to Elizabethan days. It would be delightful to think that this was the veritable scene of Shakespeare's encounter with the Dark Lady.

The Dark Lady sonnets form a group at the end of the sequence, suggesting they were obtained in a batch and added to the sequence at a later date. How they came to be united to the Southampton series is a matter of speculation, but I shall venture a possible explanation in due course.

The concluding two sonnets in this section, 153 and 154, seem in fact the earliest in date. They are distant and respectful in tone, contain no personal details, and with their talk of *holy fire of Love*, etc., suggest a newly awakened emotion. There is nothing original in these sonnets.

Matters soon advance. Sonnet 127 is in praise of dark beauty, and its attack on *art's false borrow'd face* and its praise of the mistress's genuine *black beauty* link this sonnet with 67 and 68, though the theme is something of an obsession with Shakespeare. There is, too, a personal touch in the mention of the *raven black* of the mistress's brows. In Sonnet 132 the black eyes become *mourners* over the lady's disdain and the poet's sufferings. All this is very reminiscent of *Love's Labour's Lost*. In Sonnet 128 Shakespeare touches on a subject always near his heart—music. The fair friend had been unappreciative (Sonnet 8) ; but the lady is an accomplished musician, and charms the poet by her playing while coyly refusing her kisses. Sonnet 128 is sentimental and

poor in quality : perhaps this is a sign of Shakespeare's growing
infatuation, when strong feeling was working in a manner detri-
mental to the artistic sense. Sonnet 130 is more intimate and
realistic in tone, and yet confesses to a helpless enthralment to
an object whose qualities, the poet now says, do not justify the
completeness of his enslavement :

> And yet, by heaven, I think my love as rare
> As any she belied with false compare.

Sonnet 131 reads like a reply to some angry complaint about the
tone of 130. There is an unkind defence that others say

> Thy face hath not the power to make love groan,

and the poet is rash enough to repeat that his mind assents to
this, though to his heart *thy black is fairest*. As for the lady's
black *deeds*, alluded to in this sonnet, they seem merely to be
her cruel insensibility to the pleas of her lover—nothing worse.

Next may be considered the " will " sonnets, punning on the
poet's name (surely before the fatal September of 1592 !), and a
woman's caprice, love, lust, in true Elizabethan fashion. Sonnets
135, 136, 143 all voice the poet's distress at his mistress's indifference—though 143 might conceivably belong to a later date ; the
neglect referred to here may have arisen after the lover's pleas
were answered, or may simply allude to her persistent indifference.

In Sonnet 139 the poet's cries for love become more urgent,
for the lady is a coquette, glancing aside from him (as he accuses
her of doing in Sonnet 143), while Sonnet 140 is an angry and
exasperated outburst, in which something like a threat is uttered :

> For, if I should despair, I should grow mad,
> And in my madness might speak ill of thee.

And the poet drops a hint :

> .   .   .   .   .   .   better it were,
> Though not to love, yet, love, to tell me so ;

a piece of advice which the mistress, perhaps a little frightened,
may have followed, as Sonnet 145 suggests :

> " I hate " from hate away she threw,
> And saved my life, saying—" not you."

This sonnet is defective and insipid, yet may well mark the near attainment of a passionately-sought objective, by its very flatness indicating the reaction after the tension of uncertainty. For the first time the lady shows signs of yielding.

Sonnet 151 clearly indicates the wooing is over and the mistress has yielded. It is a gross and unpleasant sonnet, when all its implications are realized. But this consummation brought the poet-lover no real happiness or satisfaction. Already there are playful recriminations which bode ill for the future, and which also suggest that not only was the poet married but also the *gentle cheater*, and that the lover's conscience was in conflict with his passion. In Sonnet 129 the full reaction to intimacy is recorded : it is a hateful experience, a *hell*, a *waste of shame*, repulsive and despised. Here we have the reaction of one to whom fulfilment brings not satisfaction but a sense of impotence and disgust—just as Shakespeare describes it in *Lucrece*. This sonnet is followed by some morbid meditations in 146 on the subject of Death, the body, and the soul, as the poet's conscience torments him. Sonnet 147 is an outburst of jealous rage, as the poet looks back with bitter resentfulness to Sonnet 132 :

> For I have sworn thee fair and thought thee bright,
> Who art as black as hell, as dark as night.

The same theme is pursued in Sonnet 141 in calmer mood, as the poet confesses his complete enslavement against the better judgment of his senses to her *that makes me sin*. Sonnet 148 continues the conflict between *eyes* and *true sight*, but there are also hints of derogatory rumours about the mistress :

> If that be fair whereon my false eyes dote,
> What means the world to say it is not so ?
>
> .   .   .   .
>
> O cunning Love ! with tears thou keep'st me blind,
> Lest eyes well-seeing thy foul faults should find.

The cry of jealousy is heard in Sonnet 150, and again there is a reference to the *true sight* that will not be believed, and to evil rumours :

> Who taught thee how to make me love thee more,
> The more I hear and see just cause of hate ?

In Sonnet 137 the jealousy culminates in a paroxysm of insults and foul accusations. The mistress is now the *bay where all men ride* (lack of proof leading to gross exaggeration, of course), and the *wide world's common place* (another almost ludicrous over-statement, if no worse). But still the poet is enthralled against his better judgment ; still the conflict between eye and true sight is maintained. What a contrast between these sonnets and those in the Southampton group, such as 54 !

Sonnet 138 is a sullen and inward acknowledgment of a compromise. Bitterly reflecting on his weakness—*my days are past the best* (how this recalls Sonnet 62 !)—the poet decides to play the farce of trust, since neither of the lovers will admit errors or deficiencies :

> And in our faults by lies we flatter'd be.

The poet has framed no definite accusation against his Dark Lady ; there is as yet only a sense of strain, an uneasy suspicion, a vague jealousy. But why does the poet dwell on his age as if he were advanced in years instead of twenty-eight or so ? Has the mistress seen and admired someone younger—the fair friend, for instance—and by some unguarded remark or gesture provoked this dismal reflection from the over-sensitive poet ? And is the poet, when he speaks in this sonnet of *truth, untutor'd youth, trust,* mentally comparing the present situation with his perfect relationship with Southampton ?

In my next group of three sonnets the situation begins to crystallize. The mistress has turned against him with a belated virtue, while at the same time *thine eyes woo* others (Sonnet 142). In the next sonnet (149) she has attempted to put the blame for her behaviour on the poet, by saying he loved her not. There is more than a mere suggestion in this sonnet that the mistress had feigned a vague jealousy of some friend of Shakespeare's as an excuse for the quarrel, for he demands in angry pain :

> Who hateth thee that I do call my friend ?

Was Southampton the friend referred to ? Had he been indifferent to the lady's advances and aroused her anger, which was then vented on the unhappy lover ? And did Shakespeare know she was in fact attracted to the clearer-sighted friend ? For he ends the sonnet thus :

> Those that can see thou lov'st, and I am blind.

Sonnet 152 renews the reproaches, but in a wearier tone. Once again may be detected the nostalgic longing for *faith, love, truth, constancy*, recalling the sonnets addressed to Southampton.

Here, for the time being, we may leave the wretched lover, his faith shaken, his mistress weary and angry, and he himself torn with bitter jealousy and painful longings for the peace that truth and faithfulness bring.

And so 1592 comes to an end.

XI.

THE POET'S SECOND ABSENCE

The theatres in London were presenting plays regularly during the winter of 1592–3, but the season came to an end in February when, as a result of an order by the Privy Council dated 28th January, 1593, all London theatres (amongst other places of amusement) were closed owing to a recrudescence of plague. There was no objection to be raised against this precaution, and Shakespeare, I believe, made none. It was only against the activities of prejudiced busybodies that he protested. The playwright, without occupation in the city and perhaps anxious to avoid encountering reminders of the painful Greene affair, may have joined a travelling company of players for a time (perhaps he was with Alleyn's company, which began a tour on 6th May, 1593), or left London on some other business.

A small group of sonnets indicates a renewed absence on the part of the poet. Here the leading image (a new one) is that of a horseman riding away, just as in the previous group the main image is that of a man haunted during the night by the appearance of his friend. It seems to me there is now a greater impression of weariness and an almost irritable grief to be traced as compared with the tone of the earlier *absence* group.

In Sonnet 50 the rider in *anger* cruelly spurs his *tired* horse as they take their *weary* way, and then is filled with remorse as the poor *beast* groans. Sonnet 51 continues the same theme. With the friend are all Shakespeare's thoughts, longings, desire ; the allusion to the desire as *of perfect'st love being made* suggests that so far the emotional relationship was unclouded by any doubts, fears or misunderstandings. There may also be implied a mental contrast between this *desire* and the infatuation described before

for the Dark Lady. At this point another link with the Dark
Lady sonnets may be mentioned. The eye-and-mind theme
occurring in those sonnets (*e.g.*, 137, 148) appears again in
Sonnet 113, which also refers to an absence :

> Since I left you, mine eye is in my mind,

But this time the theme is handled "with a difference" : it is
the *true mind* that transforms all things, the crow (a recollection
of Greene's taunt ?) and the dove alike, to beauty, to the friend's
feature. Again comes the opposition of true and untrue noted
earlier (Sonnets 137, 138, 148) in the final (emended) line :

> My most true mind thus makes mine eye untrue.

Sonnet 114 elaborates this conflict between eye and mind ;
a moment of doubt (ominous sign) whether

> Creating every bad a perfect best

is an illusion is abruptly dismissed in the concluding couplet—
the cup he drinks from :

> If it be poison'd, 'tis the lesser sin
> That mine eye loves it and doth first begin.

XII.

THE SCORN OF PRINCELY HONOURS

Sonnet 25 seems curiously disconnected from any definite
group. The constancy theme, however, allies it with the sonnets
belonging to this period. It utters a proud boast that *public
honour* and *proud titles* and martial fame are as nothing compared
with constant love between friends. Shakespeare's attitude here
is very far from one of snobbery, though he has often been accused
of that failing. Why, however, does he drag into his protestations
a reference to honours he, as he admits, is never likely to enjoy ?
And of whom is he thinking when he speaks of *princes' favourites*
and *warrior , . . foil'd* ? Perhaps it is not impossible to hazard
an answer to both questions.

The occasion of this sonnet may be connected with the rumour,
noted on 3rd May, 1593, that Southampton headed a list of four
nominees for the Order of the Garter (Lee, *Life of William*

Shakespeare, p. 313). Nothing came of this proposal during Elizabeth's lifetime, and the sonnet might be interpreted as indirect consolation for the young Earl's disappointment, on the ground that constant love is more precious and enduring than worldly and perishable glory in the gift of great princes :

> Then happy I, that love and am belov'd,
> Where I may not remove, nor be remov'd.

Thus the sonnet concludes triumphantly.

Now for the next question. My own opinion is that Shakespeare had Sir Walter Ralegh in mind. The first four lines of Sonnet 25 deal with Southampton's disappointment. Then the poet's thoughts turn to those who have enjoyed *favour*. Sir Walter had been conspicuously Elizabeth's favourite. From 1582, " honours and emoluments were showered upon him " by the Queen (Hume, *Sir Walter Ralegh*, p. 39). He had certainly spread his *fair leaves*, for " no man was so gorgeous in his attire " as Ralegh (*op. cit.*, p. 38). But a frown blighted him. He ventured all he possessed in an expedition against the Spaniards in 1592. By June of that year he was a prisoner in the Tower. The reason for his imprisonment was not given, but his relations with Elizabeth Throgmorton were the real cause of the Queen's spite. While in the Tower he wrote a pathetic letter intended for the Queen's eye. Certain lines in this letter bear an extraordinary resemblance to a passage in the sonnet. " My heart is cast into the depth of all misery," writes Ralegh, and continues, " Once amiss hath bereaved me of all. . . . All those times past—the loves, the sighs, the sorrows, the desires, can they not weigh down one frail misfortune ? " Ralegh's misery, his long unbroken successes, his *one* error, his disgrace, all seem to find an echo in these lines from the sonnet :

> The painful warrior famousèd for fight,
> After a thousand victories once foil'd,
> Is from the book of honour razèd quite,
> And all the rest forgot for which he toil'd.

Ralegh was released from the Tower, but in 1593 (the date I assign to this sonnet) and for some years after was in disgrace and forbidden to approach the Queen. There was no love lost between Ralegh and the Southampton group, for the upstart favourite and

Essex, the adored hero of Southampton, were on bad terms, and hence the allusion to Ralegh's downfall would be of special interest to the young Earl of Southampton.

XIII.

" INCONSTANT MIND "

Now come six sonnets in which lies the record of the first shadow falling on the friendship. Some rumour of happenings connected with the friend and occurring during the poet's absence has made him uneasy. The language of these sonnets does not in any way suggest there was the slightest trace of scandal attached to the incident ; and as Shakespeare does not once use the word *stain*—his usual term for sexual error—we may assume that the Dark Lady had nothing to do with the trouble. All that we are told is that the friend (and patron !) may desert the poet or may be stolen from him—*theft* is the dominant image here.

> How careful was I when I took my way,
> Each trifle under truest bars to thrust,

says the poet in Sonnet 48 ; but, he continues,

> Thou, best of dearest, and mine only care,
> Art left the prey of every vulgar thief.

The poet had merely placed the friend

> Within the gentle closure of my breast.

Was this echo of the line in the recently published *Venus and Adonis* :

> Into the quiet closure of my breast,   (*l.* 782)

a timid reminder of the nature of their association ? " Don't forget I am your poet, you my patron " seems to be the implication. And now there is danger. The friend is not locked up—only confined in the poet's loving breast :

> From whence at pleasure thou mayst come and part.
> And even thence thou wilt be stol'n, I fear,
> For truth proves thievish for a prize so dear.

Sonnet 61 expresses, with more poignancy, a similar uneasiness :

> For thee watch I, whilst thou dost wake elsewhere,
> From me far off, with others all too near.

Here for the first time the poet wonders doubtfully whether his friend's love really equals his own and can remain unshaken under the test of absence :

> O no, thy love, though much, is not so great,
> It is my love that keeps mine eye awake,
> Mine own true love . . .

In Sonnet 91 the poet expatiates on the great value he places on the friend's love :

> Thy love is better than high birth to me, . . .
> And having thee, of all men's pride I boast ;

but again the wretched fear and suspicion creep in :

> Wretched in this alone, that thou mayst take
> All this away, and me most wretched make.

In Sonnet 92 the poet, to put it colloquially, is consciously bluffing himself that the theft is impossible, for he dare not face the possibility of loss :

> But do thy worst to steal thyself away,
> For term of life thou art assurèd mine. . . .
> Thou mayst be false, and yet I know it not.

Sonnet 93 follows naturally on 92. Here the poet still hopes against hope, but the illusion is wearing thin, and a little peevishness may be traced in the last lines :

> How like Eve's apple doth thy beauty grow,
> If thy sweet virtue answer not thy show !

There is an apologetic note about the last sonnet in this group, 49. The friend may have grumbled, as he had done on a previous occasion, that he belonged to himself. The poet, in alarm, after alluding to his *defects*—ever present in his mind since the attack by Greene—admits that he must recognize :

> To leave poor me thou hast the strength of laws,
> Since why to love I can allege no cause.

There seems to be a reminiscence of Sonnet 25 pervading these sonnets.

Obviously, up to this point, the poet has no definite proofs that his friend is transferring his interest elsewhere, only fears and suspicions based on slender evidence such as haunted his relation with the Dark Lady. Not yet has the friend turned from him, but the last sonnet suggests that the friend has become restless under the inquisition and, exasperated, has claimed freedom to do as he pleases.

XIV.

A RIVAL POET — BARNABE BARNES

What, then, was the point at issue to which the above sonnets refer ? My impression is that the sonnets just discussed were the prelude to the " rival poet " theme, and have no connection with the Dark Lady situation. Some rumour, suggesting that Southampton had given his patronage to a new poet, must have reached Shakespeare's ears during his absence early in 1593. On 18th April Shakespeare's own *Venus and Adonis*, dedicated to the Earl, had been entered in the Stationers' Register. On 2nd May Alleyn's company of players, with which Shakespeare is thought to have been associated at this time, was at Chelmsford, beginning its provincial tour. And on 10th May *Parthenophil and Parthenophe* (a sequence of sonnets interspersed with madrigals, followed by elegies, odes and other types of poems) by Barnabe Barnes, whom Lee takes to be the rival poet, was entered in the Stationers' Register. This book contained dedicatory sonnets to various noblemen, the third one being addressed " To the Right Noble and virtuous Lord, HENRY, Earl of SOUTHAMPTON." Here lay the source of Shakespeare's uneasiness ! The friend was transferring his favour.

Barnes may not seem to us to be an object deserving the fear and jealousy of a Shakespeare. But we must remember that Shakespeare had so far done comparatively little to assure his place in literature, or to give him confidence in his own powers. He had just sustained a grievous wound at the hands of Greene.

Furthermore, it was like the Shakespeare of the sonnets to make a mountain out of a molehill where his affections were involved, to be hurt and tearful and filled with agonized, almost resentful, humility. The episode must be seen through the eyes of the Shakespeare of 1593, and not through the eyes of twentieth-century critics who have all the dramatist's later works spread out before them.

The assault on the rival may perhaps be taken to begin with the badly misplaced Sonnet 21. Here in a slightly contemptuous vein Shakespeare refers to some of poor Barnes' tricks of style :

> So is it not with me as with that Muse,
> Stirr'd by a painted beauty to his verse.

Barnes certainly overworks the term *Muse* (*e.g.*, Sonnets 17, 18, 45, 99 ; Madrigals 11, 18, etc.), and Shakespeare, who here employs the word for the first time, pounces on the conventional expression and hunts it to death in the subsequent sonnets. *A painted beauty* suggests a recollection of Madrigal 4 :

> My Mistress' portrait . . . .
> He 'gan with vermil, gold, white and sable
> To shadow forth . . . .

Barnes' trick of comparison, the *proud compare* of Sonnet 21 (cf. *compare to such. Proud Nature*—Barnes, Canzon 3), is next dealt with. *Sun and moon* ? Of course this refers to Barnes' lines in Sonnet 98 :

> The Sun, my Lady's Beauty represents !
> And to her virtues, the bright Moon assents.

With earth and sea's rich gems ? To be found in Sonnet 48 :

> I wish no rich refined Arabian gold !
> Nor orient Indian pearl, rare Nature's wonder !
> No diamonds . . .
> Pure pearls, with perfect rubines are inset ;
> True diamonds, in eyes ; saphires, in veins.

With April's first born flowers . . . ? We turn to Sonnet 96 :

> white lilies which combined
> With her high-smoothed brows . . . . .
> Violets from eyes, sweet blushing eglantine
> From her clear cheeks, and from her lips, sweet roses.

Or to Sonnet 58 :

> Anemone with hyacinth, Spring's pride,
> (Like to thy Beauty !) lose their lovely gloss.

Gold candles (*i.e.*, stars) ?   Look at Sonnet 95 :

> Behold (where Graces, in love's circles dance !)
> Of two clear stars, outsparkling Planets all !
> For stars, her beauty's arrow-bearers be !

The last line of Sonnet 21 is curious and a little sulky :

> I will not praise, that purpose not to sell.

Of course Barnes hoped to sell his book more profitably by claiming distinguished patronage, but is Shakespeare implying that he has no intention of publishing his own too intimate sonnets ? And is he replying to a suggestion that he should oust the more enterprising sonneteer by giving to the world the sonnets written to Southampton ?

The next " rival poet " sonnet in the sequence is 78. This alludes to Barnes' dedicatory sonnet, as Lee (*Life of William Shakespeare*, p. 317, where it is quoted in full) points out, stressing the resemblance between *taught by flight to rise* and *learned's wing* (Lee, *op. cit.*, p. 107).

Sonnet 79 is on much the same lines as Sonnet 78, with a reference to virtue (*He lends thee virtue*), recalling Barnes' *to thy virtues, of much worth.*

Lee has also pointed out (*op. cit.*, p. 108) how the " ship " metaphor of Sonnet 80 repeats a similar usage in Barnes' Sonnet 91. *A better spirit* of Shakespeare in this sonnet may be a recollection of *a prouder spirit* in Barnes' Canzon 1.

In Sonnet 83, *Speaking of worth* may be another reference to the expression in the dedicatory sonnet quoted above. The argument of Sonnet 83 is an excuse to the patron for having *slept in your report*, for *silence*—perhaps another allusion to a complaint from Southampton that his poet had failed to do him public honour with his sequence. Shakespeare does not spare his sarcasm when he describes poor Barnes' poems as a *tomb* for anyone they aim at immortalizing ! (See Madrigal 8 : *entombed in her beauty's shrine,*)

Sonnet 84 may fit in at this point, but there is another possibility which will be considered later. The apology for silence continues in Sonnet 85. (The poet in Sonnet 84 is defending himself against a charge of failing to praise, not of failing to speak.) Lee has noted, not very accurately, in connection with this sonnet, that the use of the word *hymn* for *sonnet* is peculiar to Barnes; to this may be added the repetition of the expression *spirit* and *Muse* already mentioned.

Sonnet 86, the last of the group, has given most trouble in the business of identifying the rival. Most investigators fly to Chapman as a solution. Even Lee, Barnes' stout champion, is in difficulties at this point. In a footnote (p. 109) he objects to the dragging in of Chapman, who really had no connection with Southampton at this date, to solve the problem set by *spirits,* by *compeers* (Shakespeare's only recorded use of this noun) *by night* (*cf*. Barnes' use of *compeers* in Sonnet 81), and *affable familiar ghost.* But Lee goes no further than to point out that these supernatural elements are to be found in the works of a variety of other poets. The curious thing is that Lee fails to see that one need not go outside the work of his own claimant to realize the significance of these jeering flings by Shakespeare. The *spirits* who *taught* the rival to *write,* the *compeers by night Giving him aid* may be traced to Barnes' Sestine 5 :

> .   .   .   .   .   .   in a cheerful calmy night,
>
> I call on threefold HECATE with tears !
> And here, with loud voice, invoke the Furies !
> For their assistance to me, with their furies !

And so on. Was Shakespeare to be *struck dead* by this sort of thing, or his *verse astonished* ? Was his poetry to betake itself to a *tomb* on provocation such as this ?

As for the *affable familiar ghost*—delightful phrase to modern ears !—with his nightly gulling *with intelligence,* does he not turn up in Elegy 10 ? As Barnes warbles there :

> In quiet silence of the shady night, . . .
> A lively vision, to my Fancy's sight
> Appeared . . .
> Who, softly whispering in mine ear, had told,
> " There, thou, thy fair PARTHENOPHE may see ! "

So the deluded poet thinks, and attempts to kiss the fair apparition ; but alas !

> Mistaking thee, I kissed a firebrand !
> Burnt with the fire, my senses (which did fail)
> Freshly recalled into their wits again,
> I found it was a dream !

Gulled indeed ! No wonder Shakespeare could say that such a poet and his visions

> As victors of my silence cannot boast ;
> I was not sick of any fear from thence.

To conclude the analysis of Sonnet 86, *the proud full sail* of line 1 may be a sarcastic echo of Barnes' " ship " image in his Sonnets 21, 82—*Ships winged with Winds*—and 91 ; while the image in the first two lines may have been inspired by the sensational incident of the *Great Carrack* that stirred England in September, 1592, and that was still a topic of debate as late as December, 1593 (Harrison, *Elizabethan Journal*, pp. 160, 267), or by Southampton's " Prize Ship " troubles (Stopes, *Life*, p. 52).

Lee, in the preface to his *Elizabethan Sonnets*, notes how often Barnes is echoed by Shakespeare. But the sonnets of Shakespeare referred to by Lee are early in my reckoning (22, 53, 77), and Sonnet 18 at least has a legal metaphor so common in Barnes' work. If Shakespeare's sonnets are indeed the earlier, the possibility is opened up that it is Barnes who is doing the echoing, if there is an echo. As Shakespeare's sonnets had not been published, but only at most circulated " among his private friends," as Meres notes in 1598, it may be that Southampton, through boyish pride or through carelessness, had permitted a sight of the sonnets to outsiders. This would have been an additional cause of pain to his unhappy poet, and may throw light on the lines in Sonnet 78 which imply a veiled and timid accusation :

> So oft have I invok'd thee for my Muse,
> And found such fair assistance in my verse
> As every alien pen hath got my use.

This, however, is a problem that would need much careful investigation, and I merely throw it out as a tentative suggestion.

This group of sonnets contains no clear indication how the poet's grievance was treated by the friend, or who made the first advances towards a fresh understanding. Perhaps Shakespeare accepted the rebuke that he had been too silent, and set to work on the next poem, *The Rape of Lucrece*. Southampton, who after all had never asked for or accepted Barnes' dedication, may have snubbed the aspiring poet by ignoring his bid for favour, and by telling Shakespeare not to be in a pother about nothing.

XV.

DENOUEMENT OF THE " DARK LADY " EPISODE

It may be convenient at this point to consider the final stage of the poet's entanglement with the Dark Lady. Its chronological place in the series of events depicted in the sonnets cannot be definitely determined, as in so intimate a matter support from outside evidence is naturally lacking. Judging by the general tone of the sonnets connected with this episode, we might guess that the break came in 1593 after the absence indicated by Sonnets 50 and 51 ; but there can be no certainty.

In Sonnet 144 the doubts about the Dark Lady (see X.) are resolved into something like certainty. All the blame for the situation is thrown on the *worser spirit*, the *woman colour'd ill*, who tempts the *better angel*. It is interesting, by the way, to note the derogatory use of the word *spirit*, and to compare the similar usage in the rival-poet series. Both *spirit* and *angel* are not near Shakespeare at the moment, which suggests this sonnet was written during one of Shakespeare's absences from London. Far from both, he is tormented by jealous thoughts :

> And whether that my angel be turn'd fiend,
> Suspect I may, yet not directly tell ;
> But being both from me, both to each friend,
> I guess one angel in another's hell.

Sonnet 133 pleads with the woman to spare the friend, and there is a cry of desolation :

> Of him, myself, and thee I am forsaken ;
> A torment thrice threefold thus to be cross'd.

In Sonnet 134 the poet confesses defeat ; he is compelled to yield his friend into the power of the woman. There is an interesting link between *The Merchant of Venice* and the idea in the following lines from this sonnet :

> Thou usurer, that put'st forth all to use,
> And sue a friend, came debtor for my sake.

The conclusion of the sonnet is despairingly final—*Him have I lost*.

At this point the sonnets to the woman cease. Shakespeare could hardly continue to address sonnets to his late and his friend's present mistress. How was this series, sent to the woman, added to the Southampton set ? Did the Earl come to hear of them in the course of his amour, and beg them from his new mistress ? Did he then add them to the growing pile of sonnets addressed to himself ? Some such explanation seems necessary to account for their presence in the 1609 Quarto, if Shakespeare had no hand in the publication. The Dark Lady sonnets would be kept in a separate bundle by Southampton, which would account for their appearing in a batch at the end of the sequence.

Meanwhile Shakespeare addressed half a dozen sonnets to Southampton on the same situation. In Sonnet 33 he repeats the lament, already voiced in Sonnet 144, that the friend has withdrawn himself. The withdrawal differs in nature from that spoken of in the rival poet series, for here it plainly involves a *stain* on the friend, and the word *stain* is the usual term in *Lucrece*, for instance, to denote sexual sin. As we might have expected, the poet tries to excuse his friend :

> Yet him for this my love no whit disdaineth,
> Suns of the world may stain, when heaven's sun staineth.

A more piteous tone is perceptible in Sonnet 34, though the clouds are beginning to break. The friend has begged forgiveness with tears, regretting the betrayal of his poet ; but Shakespeare's absolution is given in the spirit that pervades his final reconciliation plays, *Cymbeline* and the rest :

> Though thou repent, yet I have still the loss :
> The offender's sorrow lends but weak relief
> To him that bears the strong offence's cross.

It is an intriguing fact, by the way, that these reconciliation plays of the last period begin just about the time the Quarto first saw publication. Forgiveness is granted :

> Ah, but those tears are pearl which thy love sheds,
> And they are rich, and ransom all ill deeds.

Comfort is administered in Sonnet 35 by one eager to forgive. The very powers of reasoning are debauched to find excuses for the erring one—even to the point of rather masochistic self-accusations of favouritism.

Sonnet 40 is even more abject in tone. But an obscure criticism is revealed in the lines :

> But yet be blam'd, if thou thyself deceivest
> By wilful taste of what thyself refusest.

Does this refer to Southampton's unmarried state, to his cooling interest in the woman (Lady Bridget Manners thought Southampton too " fantastical " to make a steady husband), or to the Earl's betrayal of Shakespeare's true love while under the enchantment of the woman's false love—or to all at once ?

Sonnet 41 continues the excusing of the friend at the expense of the woman. The sestet of this sonnet has curious echoes (or premonitions) of *The Rape of Lucrece*. Tarquin (*Lucrece*, line 413) and the friend (sonnet, line 9) have both driven the rightful owner from his seat of love ; again, in *Lucrece* (line 483) and in the sonnet (lines 10–11) beauty is blamed as a temptation to sin. Finally, Tarquin's speech, especially lines 491 and 502 :

> " I see what crosses my attempt will bring, . . .
> I know repentant tears ensue the deed,"

reads much more like the sentiments of the Southampton pictured in the sonnets than like those of the traditional black tyrant of the old Roman story.

Sonnet 42 concludes the tale of this intrigue. The sentiments here are artificial, involved, and perhaps not very sincere. The argument may be summed up in the lines :

> And both for my sake lay on me this cross :
> But here's the joy ; my friend and I are one ;
> Sweet flattery ! then she loves but me alone.

With this rather cool solution to the problem, Shakespeare abandoned the theme, and settled down to do some hard work on *The Rape of Lucrece*, not forgetting to draw on his recent experiences for material. If he ever resumed sonnet-writing to the Dark Lady, after Southampton gave her up, the young Earl would naturally not be in a position to obtain the verses to add to his collection, and the poet would scarcely be the one to publish them. Perhaps Shakespeare did go back to her : if he did, this would explain a letter and *Antony and Cleopatra*. I shall deal with this matter later.

XVI.

SONNET 107 AND OTHERS — LOVE DEFIES TIME

The much-debated Sonnet 107 now presents itself for consideration. The allusions it contains promise some possibility of fixing the date when it was written, but it has been a veritable will-o'-the-wisp. Some have assigned it to 1603, others to 1599—1600 ; the latest suggestion is 1596. But none of these surmises has received more than a qualified acceptance. The tendency has been to move the date earlier and earlier in time, and I am but following a good example in attempting to do the same. I think the possibility that the sonnet was written not long after September, 1593, and perhaps in the early months (February or March ?) of 1594 cannot wholly be ruled out. In considering the allusions three points must be borne in mind. The first is that the sonnet was written after an emotional crisis in the history of the friendship, at a time when there had been a renewal of love after a dangerous threat to its continuance. The second is that the interpretation of the word *eclipse* as " grand climacteric " is not unassailable. The third is that when Shakespeare refers to political events of his day these must be seen through his eyes and not through our eyes, which have the advantage of the perspective of time.

To take the first point. Shakespeare had had *fears* of the destruction (*forfeit to a confin'd doom*) of the *true love* between himself and his friend. What better occasion could this have been than the transference of the woman's affections from poet to nobleman, following on the rival-poet incident ? So deeply was Shakespeare wounded by it that he refers to it later, in his darkest hour. Anyone might have prophesied the ending of the friendship after this trial. But Shakespeare's unusual decision (paralleled by that made by Valentine in *Two Gentlemen of Verona*) saved the friendship ; the youth was contrite (and perhaps not long constant to his stolen love), and forgiven. This sonnet, then, may well be a rapturous celebration of the renewing of love after this episode.

The *mortal moon* is undoubtedly Queen Elizabeth. But the *eclipse* may not refer to her completing safely her sixty-third year. It is by no means certain that Shakespeare gave great credence to the popular superstitions about climacterics, which depended on juggling with sevens and nines. He has already roundly stated (Sonnet 14) :

Not from the stars do I my judgment pluck,

while Hotspur, Cassius, Edmund all voice a similar scepticism. There is another possibility. In medical lore the years 45 to 60 in the life of a human being are known as the " dangerous " or " climacteric " years, and represent the period of change of life— an especially trying time in a woman's life, and one of great and perilous significance when that woman is a Queen with no natural successor. On 7th September, 1593, Elizabeth had completed her sixtieth year, and the long dangerous period of eclipse in her life had been *endured* successfully. Recent years had been full of dangers and rumours. Peter Wentworth had begun in 1587 his warnings and exhortations to put the succession in order, and had been silenced by his imprisonment in the Tower in 1593. The Queen of Scots had been executed in 1587, the Armada dispersed in 1588. More recently Elizabeth's favourite astrologer (the famous Dr. Dee), it is said (Aubrey, *Lives of Eminent Men,* Vol. II., quoted in Strickland, *Life of Queen Elizabeth,* p. 586), had warned her that she stood in danger of Lopez, her Jewish physician. But Essex, the hero of the youthful Southampton, had in January, 1594, pursued the wretched man relentlessly, and he was tried and condemned, on a charge of attempting to poison the Queen, on 28th February, 1594. On 8th February there had already been a rumour that the Queen was dead (Harrison, *Elizabethan Journal,* p. 286). The past year had been full enough of alarms and excursions, from the rumours of a Spanish invasion in February, 1593, to the latest abortive plot against the Queen's life, to give rise to many *sad augurs* besides Wentworth and Dee.

As for the *uncertainties* that *crown themselves assured,* and the enduring *peace* that is to ensue, these references may well be to something more significant in Shakespeare's eyes than in the historian's. Essex, in whom both friend and poet must have taken a deep interest, had recklessly and romantically risked his life when assisting Henry of Navarre in his struggle against the Catholic League. In July, 1593, a truce was arranged between Henry and the League, and the new king was crowned Henry IV of France on 27th February, 1594. The poet might then assume that the troubles there were to all intents and purposes ended.

As a footnote to these historical matters, a weather report may be added. From 30th March, 1594, the weather was atrocious in England (Harrison, *op. cit.*, p. 296). This lasted till 1596 ; and that period was a miserable time of high prices, famine and death owing to the failure of the harvests (Neale, *Queen Elizabeth,* p. 339 ; Chambers, *William Shakespeare*, Vol. I., p. 360). It is difficult to imagine Shakespeare describing any part of this period as a *balmy time* !

Such, then, are my reasons for suggesting late February or early March, 1594, as a possible date for this sonnet.

Turning to the latter portion of the sonnet, we find some further evidence that 1594 is a possible date. The allusions in the sestet are, I think, to *The Rape of Lucrece*, which was entered in the Stationers' Register on 9th May, 1594. The modest *poor rhyme* of the sonnet recalls the *untutored lines* of the dedication and the *wit so poor as mine* of Sonnet 26, with which the *Lucrece* dedication has so often been compared. *Tyrants' crests* is an image which would naturally occur to Shakespeare while writing about Tarquin, a tyrant in more senses than one. (Compare *the tyranny of the king* in the argument to *Lucrece*.) It is not clear what Shakespeare was thinking of when he used the expression *tombs of brass*. He had referred to Barnes' poetic efforts as a *tomb* (Sonnet 83). He might have been thinking of the splendid metal screen decorating the tomb of Henry VII in Westminster Abbey. Or was he already meditating the subject of *Romeo and Juliet*, and vaguely picturing his golden monument that was to commemorate the love of the incomparable pair ? Both Broke and Paynter, Shakespeare's sources, mention only a marble tomb or monument. And this possibility leads one to reflect that *Romeo and Juliet*, the first play in which the genius of Shakespeare spreads its wings, may have been written during the flush of rapture following the reconciliation between the poet and his friend. Perhaps it was regarded by the two as specifically

Southampton's play; and, if there are any grounds for this surmise, a strange and tragic light is thrown on some later developments.

Sonnet 107 has considered the impotence of time to affect love. The same thought occurs in Sonnet 115. In fact Time has brought Love to fuller perfection; the *tyranny* (compare *tyrants' crests* above) that brings all earthly things to ruin has been impotent against the power of love, now even deeper than in the springtime of the friendship.

Sonnet 116, with its magnificent defiance of time, change and separation, follows naturally on 115.

Where Sonnet 122 should be placed is uncertain, but the apology for giving away a gift of *tables* includes the argument that love needs no reminders, but can endure without them :

Beyond all date, even to eternity.

The connection between the thought of this sonnet and that of 116 is close.

Sonnet 123 is linked with the preceding one by the strong emphasis on the " I " in the first line :

No, Time, thou shalt not boast that I do change.

Were these protestations called forth by Southampton's growing jealousy of his poet's absorption in his profession ? Chambers (*William Shakespeare*, Vol. I., p. 270) credits 1594–5 with three plays (and there may have been more) : a large number, never exceeded in any year of the poet's activities and equalled only once—the 1599–1600 effort. Are the *pyramids* his plays, *dressings of a former sight* ? And was the image suggested by the four marble obelisks at the four corners of the Southampton tomb ? (See photograph in Stopes, *Life of Southampton*, facing p. 6.)

Fresh assurances of devotion follow in Sonnet 124. The reference to

. . . . thrallèd discontent,
Whereto the inviting time our fashion calls,

seems to indicate there were several serious and similar manifestations of political discontent at the time. And this is true of early 1594. Essex had unearthed the alleged double plot against the lives of the Queen and Don Antonio of Portugal, as I have said previously. There was also another plot against the Queen— that of Captain Jacques, mentioned by Harrison (*Elizabethan*

Journal, p. 283) under the date 4th February 1594, while there was a scare that the Tower was going to be burned, which Harrison (*op. cit.*, p. 284) notes in an entry dated 6th February, 1594.

The curious and rather baffling Sonnet 125 seems to hint at further complaints, based on jealousy, from the young Earl. The *suborn'd informer*—there were plenty of informers at this time !—recalls, perhaps with intent, the *sour informer*, Jealousy, of *Venus and Adonis* (line 655), to which passage Shakespeare may have wished to refer his patron. Shakespeare assures him, it appears, that no ambitions (as dramatist ?) would be allowed to interfere with his affectionate service to his friend. The allusion to *great bases for eternity* strengthens the impression that by the *pyramids* of Sonnet 123 he meant his plays. No, far from neglecting his friend, he has ready his *oblation, poor but free* (*poor* again, by the way) to offer him. It is a

> . . . . . mutual render, only me for thee.

The *oblation* was *The Rape of Lucrece*, finished in the early months of 1594 : *What I have done is yours ; . . . being part in all I have, devotedly yours.*

The poem was presented, I think, with Sonnet 32 as a sort of covering letter to the patron.

> These poor rude lines of thy deceased lover

strikes the very note of the prose dedication : *My untutored lines . . . the love I dedicate to your lordship . . . to whom I wish long life.* In both sonnet and dedication is revealed a sense of inferiority. The prose passage runs : *Were my worth greater, my duty would show greater ; meantime, as it is, it is bound to your lordship.* The sonnet has :

> Had my friend's Muse grown with this growing age,
> A dearer birth than this his love had brought,
> To march in ranks of better equipage :
> But since he died, and poets better prove,
> Theirs for their style I'll read, his for his love.

XVII.

THE RAPE OF LUCRECE

The subject matter of Shakespeare's *Lucrece* shows many affinities with situations already traced in this study. Collatine, the *dear friend* of his *superior*, Tarquin, boasts of his wife, and awakens the tyrant's desire for

> This earthly saint, adorèd by this devil
>
> (line 85).

(Compare Sonnet 144.) Tarquin experiences agonies of indecision before the deed, by which, like a *foul usurper*, he plans *From this fair throne to heave the owner out* (line 413 ; *cf.* Sonnet 41). The beauty of Lucrece is blamed as the cause of the crime (line 483 ; *cf.* Sonnet 41). Tarquin sees *what crosses my attempt will bring* (line 491 ; *cf.* Sonnet 42), and knows *repentant tears ensue the deed* (line 502 ; *cf.* Sonnet 34). Lucrece begs him earnestly, *Mud not the fountain that gave drink to thee* (line 577 ; *cf.* Sonnet 35), and refers to his youth thus :

> How will thy shame be seeded in thine age,
> When thus thy vices bud before thy spring ?
>
> (lines 603–4).

Young Tarquin, young friend. Tarquin, however, is determined and has his *will*, only to experience the familiar Shakespearian reaction to the satisfaction of illicit love—disgust, weakness and shame (*cf.* Sonnet 147). Lucrece's meditations after his departure include some reflections on the power of time to *ruinate* and *fill with wormholes stately monuments* (line 946 ; *cf.* Sonnet 64). She is haunted by the *stain* (*cf.* Sonnet 33) to her honour, but, contemplating a handsome tapestry depicting the fall of Troy, realizes :

> It easeth some, though none it ever cur'd,
> To think their dolour others have endured
>
> (lines 1581–2).

The reflection may throw some light on Shakespeare's reason for choosing this subject. It may be noted that Lucrece shows particular animosity against Helen : *Show me the strumpet that began this stir* (line 1471)—an odd remark from one whose own experience might have taught her more charity towards the woman in the case, but a sentiment admirably suited to the Shakespeare of the Dark Lady sonnets.

Many more parallels between *Lucrece* and the sonnets may be drawn, but there are also curious reminiscences of the style affected by Barnes in his *Parthenophil and Parthenophe*. Shakespeare seems to go out of his way to imitate (or can it be to guy ?) the worst hyperbole of Barnes. Lucrece's eyes are *those fair suns set in her . . . sky* (line 1230) ; they drop the *brinish pearl* (line 1213), while the country vignettes of *Venus and Adonis* yield to masses of classical allusions in the style of the *learned* one.

The Rape of Lucrece was entered in the Stationers' Register on 9th May, 1594, and was published with a dedication to Southampton, a dedication that, it has often been noted, bears a remarkable resemblance to Sonnet 26. In the sonnet, as in the dedication, Shakespeare insists on his *duty*, of which the *written embassage* is a token. Was the writing of this poem an effort, which only a strong sense of duty made possible ?

Southampton evidently received the poem with pleasure, and found it *worthy perusal* ; Sonnet 38 reads like a modest reply to his expressions of delighted surprise, though it also contains what may look like some sarcastic digs at the not yet forgotten (or forgiven ?) impudence of Barnes :

> Thine own sweet argument, too excellent
> For every vulgar paper to rehearse.
>
> .   .   .   .
>
> For who's so dumb that cannot write to thee,
> When thou thyself dost give invention light ?

We have heard of the *dumb* before in Sonnet 78 ! The use of the term *Muse* in this sonnet may also point to another sarcastic hit at the enemy.

> If my slight Muse do please these curious days

seems like a half-contemptuous reference to his popularity as a poet.

Sonnets 73 and 74 mark a relapse into some morbid meditations, characteristic of Shakespeare when suffering from the reaction after a strain. He dwells, with more sincerity (perhaps with more justification now) than is to be found in the earlier sonnet on the same subject, on his age, contrasting his present more sober outlook—*ashes*—with the *fire* of his more youthful days (Sonnet 73). Is he thinking of the amorous *Venus and Adonis* and the lush sonnets he poured out at the beginning of the friendship, and comparing them with his present efforts ? He acknowledges gently the love so enthusiastically affirmed by the grateful dedicatee of *Lucrece*, and in Sonnet 74 reflects that when the *fell arrest* occurs the friend will still possess *the better part of me* as a memorial. *This line* may refer to *Lucrece*, or to the line of dedication that accompanied the poem. Perhaps, too, his thoughts turn to Marlowe, the *dead shepherd*, the only poet whose lines Shakespeare directly quotes and one who shared with him the savage blows of Greene.

<blockquote>The coward conquest of a wretch's knife</blockquote>

might easily be a reference to the sordid tragedy of Marlowe's death on 30th May, 1593, when he was stabbed by Frizer. Marlowe was two months older than Shakespeare.

The gloomy fit may also have been inspired by the brief resurrection of an unpleasant memory. *Greene's Funerals*, entered in the Stationers' Register on 1st February, 1594, appeared in print with the unkind allusion to Shakespeare in the *Groats-worth of Wit* repeated (Chambers, *William Shakespeare*, Vol. II., p. 190). Incidentally, the publication of this work was, says the printer of it, " contrary to the author's expectation." The offensive passage runs as follows :

<blockquote>
Greene, is the ground of every painter's die,
Greene, gave the ground, to all that wrote upon him.
Nay more the men, that so eclips'd his fame :
Purloin'd his Plumes, can they deny the same ?
</blockquote>

XVIII.

THE POET'S THIRD ABSENCE

1594 was a year of change to Strange's Men. On 16th April they lost their patron by death. They were, however, at Winchester on 16th May, under the Countess's name. In June a new company appears, the Lord Chamberlain's Men. This company performed at Newington Butts from 3rd June to 13th

June. After that they are recorded as performing at Marlborough in September. The touring period over, they settled in London for a stay which seems to have been uninterrupted throughout 1595, until the plague intervened the next year and a Privy Council minute of 22nd July, 1596, temporarily prohibited the presentation of plays in the city of London (Chambers: *William Shakespeare*, Vol. I., p. 64 ; *Elizabethan Stage*, Vol. II., p. 193 ; Vol. IV., p. 319). By the end of 1594 we know for certain that Shakespeare was a prominent member of the Lord Chamberlain's Company. Perhaps Shakespeare's rise may be connected with the story that Southampton gave him a thousand pounds—to buy a share, we may surmise, in the new company. If he did give his poet a thousand pounds (Chambers suggests the actual sum was more probably a hundred), it may have been a magnificent and unparalleled coming-of-age gift on 6th October, 1594, from the patron to his poet. Southampton was capable of a gesture of fantastical extravagance, and the relationship was no ordinary one. One wonders if the harping on a thousand pounds in *Henry IV*. has any connection with this episode ! If the tale of the gift is true, Southampton had reason to feel jealous, as it has been suggested he did, when he saw his poet becoming immersed in theatrical affairs. On the other hand, Southampton was in financial difficulties about the time of his twenty-first birthday, for he had had to pay Lady Elizabeth Vere the huge sum of five thousand pounds for breach of promise before he could free himself from that entanglement.

To return to the sonnets. There are renewed indications that the poet was absent, perhaps travelling with Strange's Men, perhaps with the Lord Chamberlain's, perhaps on his own business. In this group the poet plays with the image of *winter* to symbolize the sorrows of separation.

Sonnet 98 states clearly that the poet was absent from his friend in the spring :

> When proud-pied April dress'd in all his trim
> Hath put a spirit of youth in every thing.

Yet, laments the poet—

> Yet seem'd it winter still, and, you away,
> As with your shadow I with these did play.

Does this allude to the absence during the spring tour of Strange's Men ? And what is the *summer's story* the poet failed to tell ? Is this a figure of speech, or an admission he had been unable to begin a new poem, perhaps in honour of his friend's coming-of-age ?

Sonnet 56 is an address to Love not to become satiated or to relapse into a state of *perpetual dullness*. The *sad interim* should be a bond, like the ocean joining continents, or like winter, that sharpens the longing for summer.

The *winter* of *absence* in Sonnet 97 seems to refer to another separation, occurring in the late summer and autumn ; it would tally with the tour of the Lord Chamberlain's Men.

A pair of sonnets expressing a related idea, and with similar opening phrases, may be considered here.

In Sonnet 52, beginning

> So am I as the rich, whose blessed key,

the poet consoles himself for the infrequency with which the friends meet by reflecting that this makes for the greater enjoyment of the *sweet up-lockèd treasure* when the chance does come.

Sonnet 75 begins :

> So are you to my thoughts as food to life,

echoing, too, the *feasts* of the previous sonnet. But here the poet is less confident that he has complete control over his *treasure* ; there is anxiety whether the *filching age will steal* it, and perhaps a shade of reproachful suspicion in the lines :

> Sometime all full with feasting on your sight,
> And by and by clean starvèd for a look.

Did anything happen in 1594 to cause a strained feeling between Shakespeare and his patron ? Had another Barnabe Barnes come on the scene ?

XIX.

ANOTHER RIVAL — NASH

There *was* another rival. The villain of the piece this time was Thomas Nash, a far more important literary figure than Barnes. On 7th September, 1593, Nash's book *The Unfortunate*

Traveller, or The Life of Jack Wilton was entered in the Stationers' Register, but was not published till the next year, when it paraded an eloquent dedication to Southampton. Shakespeare, I am certain, did not allow the incident to pass unregarded ; he fired two sonnets at the innocent young Earl, for whom, by this time, one begins to experience a certain sympathy in his troubles.

Nash, in his dedication, has these passages : " All that in this fantastical treatise I can promise is some reasonable conveyance of history, and variety of mirth. . . . A new brain, a new wit, a new style, a new soul will I get me to canonize your name to posterity if in this my first attempt I be not taxed of presumption. Of your gracious favour I despair not, for I am not altogether Fame's outcast." (The last sentence, by the way, suggests that the dedication had not received Southampton's sanction, and was, indeed, nothing more than an unauthorized bid for patronage.)

In Sonnet 76, Shakespeare, in his comment on this piece of audacity, seizes on the boasts of *variety* and *new* powers :

> Why is my verse so barren of new pride,
> So far from variation or quick change ?
> Why with the time do I not glance aside
> To new-found methods and to compounds strange ?

Nash's fourfold repetition of *new* is paralleled by Shakespeare's further uses of the word—*dressing old words new* and *daily new and old.* The glance at the *new-found methods* reminds us that Nash's book really was something new in English literature— an original prose romance with a lively comic element. There had been translations of the picaresque novel into English before this, as Jusserand points out (*The English Novel in the Time of Shakespeare*, p. 294) ; but Nash and his fellows were the first to introduce a vein of native realistic humour into English prose fiction.

Shakespeare, in the fourth line of this sonnet, alludes to *compounds strange.* Jusserand (*op. cit.*, pp. 303–4) points out as a peculiarity of Nash's style that he " coins at need new words or fetches them from classical or foreign languages," and considers he " cannot always avoid the ordinary defects of this particular style." He goes on to quote (*op. cit.*, p. 306) Nash's preface to his *Christ's Tears over Jerusalem*, added to the 1594 edition, as follows : " To the second rank of reprehenders, that

complain of my boisterous compound words . . . thus I reply :
That no wind that blows strong but is boisterous. . . . For the
compounding of my words, therein I imitate rich men. . . . Our
English tongue of all languages most swarmeth with the single
money of monosyllables, which are the only scandal of it."

Why write I still all one . . . . . . ?

asks Shakespeare in monosyllables, and punning.

Sonnet 108 bears a remarkable resemblance to another and
earlier argument launched by Nash. In his *Anatomy of Absurdity*
(1589) Nash had attacked the rehashing of old themes : " What
else, I pray you," he asks, " do these Babel book-mongers
endeavour but to repair the ruinous walls of Venus' court, to
restore to the world that forgotten legendary licence of lying,
to imitate afresh the fantastical dreams of those exiled Abbey-
lubbers from whose idle pens proceeded those worn-out impres-
sions. . . .," etc. A fine thing for the author of *Venus and
Adonis* and the great borrower of plots to read !

In Sonnet 108, it seems to me, Shakespeare manages to
combine an attack on Nash's theories of art, a defence of himself
and his methods, a compliment to his friend and a rather pathetic
reminder of their love :

> What's new to speak, what new to register,
> That may express my love or thy dear merit ?

he asks. Nothing, he answers, and continues :

> . . . eternal love in love's fresh case
> Weighs not the dust and injury of age,
>
> .   .   .   .
>
> But makes antiquity for aye his page,
> Finding the first conceit of love there bred
> Where Time and outward form would show it dead.

The phrase used in this sonnet, *hallow'd thy fair name*, is, incidentally, almost a repetition of Nash's *canonize your name* quoted
above. In fact, the resemblances between these two sonnets and
Nash's dedication and prefaces are numerous and striking ; I
cannot help feeling that the two are linked. The word *Muse*,
associated with the onslaught on Barnes, is not employed here,
nor is there anything in Sonnets 76 and 108 to make them
inapplicable to a prose writer and his works.

What steps Southampton took to soothe the wounded feelings of his poet we do not know. But it is significant that in the second edition of *The Unfortunate Traveller* the offending dedication was withdrawn. This second edition appeared in the same year as the first—1594 ; and the book was never again reprinted till modern times. Furthermore, the new edition was said to be " newly corrected and augmented." Yet apart from two minor alterations the two editions do not materially differ—except in the omission of the dedication. I think a quite plausible explanation of these facts is that Southampton, inspired by Shakespeare, objected to the dedication, with the result that a new issue of *The Unfortunate Traveller* was prepared with the dedication omitted.

XX.

WILLOBIE HIS AVISA

Now come a pair of sonnets, 36 and 88, adumbrating a curious situation. Some scandal or *guilt—blots*—had been attached to the poet's good name. This is the theme of Sonnet 36. Shakespeare feels it better that he and Southampton should be *twain*, though this makes no difference to their steadfast love. His fear is that by association the *blots* may compromise the good name of his patron. Some incident affecting both their *lives* makes separation advisable, and there is a hint that Shakespeare can offer Southampton no more dedications, lest this draw further attention to their connection :

> I may not evermore acknowledge thee,
> Lest my bewailèd guilt should do thee shame,
> Nor thou with public kindness honour me,
> Unless thou take that honour from thy name :
> But do not so ; I love thee in such sort
> As, thou being mine, mine is thy good report.

The painful sacrifice, the poet feels, must be made.

Sonnet 88 gives some further curious details. It is not, I think, symptomatic of any quarrel, but simply an assurance of the poet's trustworthiness under the extremest pressure. Even if the friend were to join in the attack, the poet will protect him at his own expense (*cf.* Sonnet 35). Yet the friend was really implicated in the matter, and the rumours have a foundation of fact :

> Upon thy side against myself I'll fight,
> And prove thee virtuous, though thou art forsworn.

(For *forsworn* compare Sonnet 41.) Fortunately, however, the full and true facts are evidently not known, and so far the friend has escaped the most damning discoveries of the gossipers ; and Shakespeare is able to say :

> Such is my love, to thee I so belong,
> That for thy right myself will bear all wrong.

To what could Shakespeare have been alluding ? I think that a ghost from the painful past had arisen, and that these two sonnets may be connected with the appearance of *Willobie His Avisa*, entered in the Stationers' Register on 3rd September, 1594, and published in the same year. It is not necessary here to go into the details of the story in *Willobie*. The identification of " W.S.", the " old player," with Shakespeare has often been made, and the direct allusions to the recently published *Lucrece* in the prefatory verses strengthen the case. In the advice on how to make love, given by W.S. to H.W., there are more echoes from Shakespeare's plays than critics seem to have realized. Most of the parallels are to be discovered in *Two Gentlemen of Verona* and *Titus Andronicus*. Out of many, two passages from the plays may be compared with two passages from *Willobie*. Valentine's advice to the Duke in *Two Gentlemen* runs as follows :

> Win her with gifts, if she respect not words.
> Dumb jewels often, in their silent kind,
> More than quick words, do move a woman's mind.
>
> . . . .
> If she do frown, 'tis not in hate of you.
>
> . . . .
> Take no repulse, whatever she doth say ;
> For " get you gone," she doth not mean " away ! "
> Flatter, and praise, commend, extol their graces ;
> Though ne'er so black, say they have angels' faces.
>
> (*Two Gentlemen of Verona*, III., i.)

c

Now for W.S.'s advice to H.W. :

> At first repulse you must not faint,
> Nor fly the field though she deny
> You twice or thrice   .   .   .   .   .
> .   .   .   .
> Apply her still with divers things
> (For gifts the wisest will deceive),
> Sometimes with gold, sometimes with rings.
> .   .   .   .
> You must commend her loving face,
> For women joy in beauty's praise.
> .   .   .   .
> When she doth frown, you must be sad.

The second parallel is particularly interesting. Dr. Spurgeon, in her study of *Shakespeare Imagery* (pp. 112–3), says that the *stopped oven* image is almost peculiar to this writer. Something like it is employed in *Two Gentlemen*, I. ii. :

> Fire that's closest kept burns most of all.

Titus Andronicus, II. v., has

> Sorrow concealèd, like an oven stopp'd,
> Doth burn the heart to cinders where it is.

The words of W.S. are almost a repetition :

> The smother'd flame, too closely pent,
> Burns more extreme for want of vent.
> So sorrows shrin'd in secret breast
> Attaint the heart with hotter rage
> Than griefs that are to friends express'd.

Now compare *Venus and Adonis* (lines 331–4) :

> An oven that is stopp'd, or river stay'd,
> Burneth more hotly, swelleth with more rage :
> So of concealèd sorrow may be said ;
> Free vent of words love's fire doth assuage.

If this is a coincidence, it is a remarkable one. The image was not used by Shakespeare after *Willobie* appeared.

Did Willobie get hold of some garbled story of the Dark Lady intrigue, and, not knowing the full facts, associate it with the story of *chaste* Lucrece, thinking that that poem was meant to shadow forth the poet's own tale ? It was a trick of the time to read contemporary meanings into any literary production. Nash himself protested against this kind of thing in his preface to *Christ's Tears over Jerusalem* (ed. 1594) : " I am informed," he says, " there be certain busy wits abroad . . . that scorn to be counted honest, plain-meaning men, like their neighbours, for not so much as out of mutton and potage, but they will construe a meaning of kings and princes. Let one but name bread, but they will interpret it to be the town of Breda in the Low Countries."

Now we can imagine, when the tale of *Willobie His Avisa*, with its pointed references to Shakespeare ; its ambiguous allusion to St. George's Inn (Newington Butts or Southwark ?), " where captain's cry Victorious land, to conquering rage " (pointing to Talbot's cry in *Henry VI., Part I.*, IV. vi. : " Saint George and victory. . . . The regent hath . . . left us to the rage of France his sword " ?) ; its presentation of Henry Willobie (Willow—despairing lover—Wriothesley ?), who was " suddenly infected with the contagion of a fantastical fit " (*fantastical* was Lady Bridget Manners' description of Southampton when she declined to consider him as a possible husband, according to a letter written 5th July, 1594, and quoted by Mrs. Stopes in her *Life of Southampton*, p. 66), and consulted his " familiar friend W.S."—we can imagine how, when this book appeared in print, the two friends must have glanced apprehensively at each other on receiving this unpleasant reminder of an uncomfortable episode in their joint lives. That the author of *Willobie His Avisa* mistakenly thought that Avisa was virtuous was thanks to *Lucrece*, with its insistence on the chastity of the heroine, but even then the story was humiliating and discreditable ; and the true facts, so peculiar and even disgraceful, might come out at any moment —especially if " Avisa " talked. She didn't, it appears, and who knows whether *Antony and Cleopatra* was not Shakespeare's *amende* to this coquette, wavering, false, fascinating, yet in the end splendidly loyal to her older lover ?

Willobie His Avisa was immensely popular, went through seven editions, and occasioned plenty of gossip and comment. The second edition appeared in 1596, the year of the break between Shakespeare and Southampton, according to my scheme. A third was issued in 1599, but after Southampton had been released from the Tower this edition was called in by the High Commission, on 4th June. The High Commission saw, or was inspired to see, something scandalous in the book—and this, too, in spite of an elaborate explanation, given evidently in the 1596 edition, that Avisa was a purely imaginary character. Why this protestation from the author ? Had things been made hot meanwhile for the busybody ? And had Southampton's release anything to do with the suppression ? It is also interesting to note that the fifth edition appeared in 1609, the year in which the sonnets were published. A new edition came out in 1635, when both Shakespeare and Southampton were dead.

The general circumstances surrounding the actual Dark Lady episode, and the unwelcome appearance of the inaccurate *Willobie His Avisa*, seem to me to fit the tenor of the two sonnets discussed in this section. I do not wish it to be thought that I insist that they do refer to this episode, but I think the accumulation of evidence makes the suggestion worth considering.

XXI.

THE DANVERS AFFAIR

There was to be yet another upheaval before 1594 closed. Southampton's rash, generous, *fantastical* nature involved him in a queer bit of indiscretion. The story is told in full in Mrs. Stopes' life of Southampton (Chapter VII.). The facts are briefly these. There had been bad blood between the Danvers family and a neighbour, and the quarrel had even involved the servants of the two households. On Friday, 4th October, 1594, Sir Charles Danvers and his brother, Sir Henry, had forced their way into a house where their enemies were dining, and in the scuffle that ensued had killed, more or less accidentally, one of the members of the Long family. Southampton, though not in any way implicated in the actual crime, had assisted the Danvers brothers, who were his friends, to escape. A considerable amount of gossip and scandal attached to the young Earl's name. This was aggravated when, in January, 1595, an inquiry was held into the circumstances of the murder and of the escape.

Sonnet 69 seems to me to refer to this incident. It speaks of the universal praise accorded to Southampton's external beauty, but adds that the praisers, judging by the friend's *deeds*, put a *rank* interpretation on his *mind*. There is a plain rebuke in the concluding couplet to the effect that Southampton is beginning to associate with undesirable characters, though there is no suggestion that he is in reality guilty of any misdoing :

> But why thy odour matcheth not thy show,
> The soil is this, that thou dost common grow.

Indeed, Sonnet 70 expressly exonerates the friend from any accusation of ill-doing, whatever appearances may suggest :

> For slander's mark was ever yet the fair.

Two lines seem to point to the sonnet's having been written after Southampton's coming of age :

> And thou present'st a pure, unstainèd prime.
> Thou hast pass'd by the ambush of young days.

Was, by the way, the

> . . . crow that flies in heaven's sweetest air

—that bird of ill omen to Shakespeare—to which he alludes in line 4 of this sonnet, the result of a rankling memory of his own ordeal at the hands of the slanderous Greene ? It will be noticed, too, that there are hints of *Romeo and Juliet* in the Danvers episode. Mercutio is killed in much the same way as the Danvers' victim, Henry Long, and the servants of the two houses are involved in real life and in the play. Neither element is found in Shakespeare's sources.

The theme of these two sonnets seems to suit well with the circumstances of the Danvers affair. The reference to the coming of age, past but not long past, is also appropriate in point of time, and leads naturally to the next sonnet to be considered.

XXII.

SONNET 104

The reference to the friend's age in Sonnet 70 :

> Thou hast pass'd by the ambush of young days,

may have provoked some melancholy comment from Southampton to the effect that indeed he was growing old, and could no longer be considered a *sweet boy*, as Shakespeare had styled him in Sonnet 108. The poet hastened to provide reassurance, and it is here that I place Sonnet 104, the " three years " sonnet.

This sonnet begins with a reference to winter, which suggests that it was written during that season—perhaps the cold month of January or February when the Danvers affair was reaching its climax. This carries the dating back to the summer of 1592. The next reference to the *three beauteous springs* takes the meeting still further back to the spring of 1592, and the three Aprils make it impossible to place the meeting later than April, 1592, though it easily have occurred a month or so earlier. If this sonnet was written to commemorate the third anniversary of the meeting, that encounter may have taken place in January or February, 1592, as has been my impression from other evidence.

In this sonnet Shakespeare insists on only one feature of the friend that has remained unchanged during the three years, the feature that he celebrated in the first stages of their friendship—the young Earl's beauty. Southampton may well have felt that he had other qualities deserving mention and appreciation. (He was *fond on praise*, we shall hear later !) He had bitterly regretted, to the point of tears, the Dark Lady episode ; he had stood by his friend in the Greene business ; he had neither solicited nor accepted the various dedications that had been thrust on him by other writers, but had bestowed the honour of his *public kindness* on Shakespeare alone, and was prepared to do so again, in spite of the Willobie affair. There were also other favours. Perhaps one of them had led to Shakespeare's prominent position in the Lord Chamberlain's Company, and had given him the opportunity of playing before the great Elizabeth herself at Greenwich (along with such famous actors as Kempe and Burbage) during the Christmas season of 1594.

Sonnet 105 makes prompt and full amends for the neglect. The devotion of the patron to the poet is reciprocated. The poet and his verse are vowed to one and to one alone. And it is not only the beauty of the friend that has called forth this adoration. Kindness and truth are ranked now with beauty as the supreme qualities making up a perfect whole :

> " Fair, kind, and true " have often liv'd alone,
> Which three till now never kept seat in one.

XXIII.

" O TRUANT MUSE "

Meanwhile time was passing. This spring there was no poem ready for dedication to Southampton and publication. We can imagine the patron complaining a trifle testily : " You will not allow others to dedicate their work to me, and we obviously cannot think of publishing the sonnets. No poem ; nothing but plays and acting and theatrical business the whole time. What sort of figure as a patron do I cut in these circumstances ? " Shakespeare was conscience-stricken and apologized. He had been occupied lately in writing *Romeo and Juliet,* and using matter suggested by the Danvers affair ; but he felt the force of Southampton's complaint.

Sonnet 100 is a rebuke directed at his dilatory Muse for wasting her time thus :

> Where art thou, Muse, that thou forget'st so long
> To speak of that which gives thee all thy might ?
> Spend'st thou thy fury on some worthless song
> Darkening thy power to lend base subjects light ?
> Return, forgetful Muse, and straight redeem
> In gentle numbers time so idly spent.

The Muse is urged in hopeful tones to survey *my love's sweet face* for inspiration, and to celebrate his beauty.

Sonnet 101 is another invocation to the *truant Muse,* but reads as if Shakespeare had suddenly remembered an earlier objection to his habit of concentrating on the element of beauty to the neglect of other qualities in his friend. For the emphasis here is hastily thrown on *truth—truth in beauty dyed*. The Muse is reproached :

> Because he needs no praise, wilt thou be dumb ?
> Excuse not silence so ; for't lies in thee
> To make him much outlive a gilded tomb.

Had Shakespeare in his mind, when he penned this last line, the statues *in pure gold* that were to immortalize the names of Romeo and of Juliet ?

Things did not go well. Inspiration would not work to order, and there was nothing fit to offer the patron. Sonnet 102 is full of apologies and ingenuous excuses :

> My love is strengthen'd, though more weak in seeming ;
> I love not less, though less the show appear :
> That love is merchandiz'd whose rich esteeming
> The owner's tongue doth publish every where.
>
> . . . .
> . . . . . . I sometime hold my tongue,
> Because I would not dull you with my song.

Sonnet 103 is positively a wail on the subject of the poet's impotence :

> Alack, what poverty my Muse brings forth,
>
> . . . .
> O blame me not if I no more can write !
> Look in your glass . . . .
>
> . . . .
> . . . more, much more, than in my verse can sit
> Your own glass shows you when you look in it.

And with that the patron had to be content, it seems.

XXIV.

YET ANOTHER RIVAL — MARKHAM

If Shakespeare could do nothing to celebrate his friend's shining qualities, all poets were not so impotent, and in the course of 1595 an egregious flatterer appeared on the scene with a poem and a dedication to work havoc in gentle Shakespeare's bosom, and, I believe, to provoke another pair of sonnets.

On 9th September, 1595, the poem, *The Most Honourable Tragedy of Sir Richard Grinvile, Knight,* by Gervase Markham, was entered " under the Warden's Hands ". Markham dedicated this poem to Southampton in a sonnet remarkable for its bad taste and high-flown style. In it he praises the Earl in strained and exaggerated terms as

> Thou glorious Laurel of the Muses' hill.

Markham begs his patron :

> From graver subjects of thy grave assays
> Bend thy courageous thoughts unto these lines,

and implores him when the poem appears

> . . . to sweet it with thy blessèd tongue,
> Whose well-tun'd sound stills music in the spheres ;
> So shall my tragic lays be blest by thee,
> And from thy lips suck their eternity.

In this ridiculous, not to say blasphemous, manner did Markham address his patron.

Shakespeare, I think, made reference to this incident in two sonnets usually grouped with the earlier rival-poet series. Now Shakespeare is most precise in his language and thought. He does not muddle ideas. In these sonnets, 84 and 82, he is saying something that he does not mention in the other sonnets on the Barnabe Barnes topic. He is saying not that the praise is exaggerated and fanciful, but that it is downright bad in taste and false in style—criticisms that Markham well deserved for his vulgarity.

Sonnet 84 holds up to scorn the absurd exaggeration of expression in the rival, and defends Shakespeare's own moderation :

> Let him but copy what in you is writ,
> Not making worse what nature made so clear.

The sonnet ends rather snappishly with a positive rebuke to the patron for encouraging this sort of rubbish :

> You to your beauteous blessings add a curse,
> Being fond on praise, which makes your praises worse.

Blessings—no doubt a fling at Markham's *blessed tongue* and *blest by thee* !

There were bound to be repercussions. Shakespeare was told by the incensed friend that in view of his own recent failure to produce anything to patronize, he had no right to raise any objections to the friend's bestowing his interest elsewhere. Shakespeare admits the truth of this argument in Sonnet 82, and offers a dignified apology :

> I grant thou wert not married to my Muse,
> And therefore mayst without attaint o'erlook
> The dedicated words which writers use
> Of their fair subject, blessing every book.

Blessing again ! And the change to the formal *thou* !

> Thou art as fair in knowledge as in hue,

Shakespeare continues, remembering the *grave assays* admired by the rival. But, unmoved by the compliment presumably directed at him in the second line of Markham's sonnet to the patron :

> Whose eyes doth crown the most victorious pen,

he sticks to his criticism of the *strainèd touches rhetoric can lend*. Let the friend enjoy this sort of thing, if he thinks he merits it, but he will hear only *plain words* from his *true-telling friend* :

> And their gross painting might be better used
> Where cheeks need blood ; in thee it is abused.

So the episode closed.

XXV.

A LOVER'S COMPLAINT

While Shakespeare was becoming more and more absorbed in theatrical affairs and losing touch with his friend, the young Earl began to look elsewhere for companionship. Gossip was linking his name with that of Elizabeth Vernon, cousin to Essex, and a letter quoted by Mrs. Stopes (*Life of Southampton*, p. 86) records on 23rd September, 1595, the rumour that " My Lord of Southampton doth with too much familiarity court the fair Mistress Vernon."

Shakespeare must have heard these stories, and, greatly concerned, perhaps not a little jealous, rushed on his doom with good advice and warnings. Sonnets 95, 96 and 94 clearly point to some scandal in which the friend is implicated. Unlike those sonnets connected with the Danvers affair, these indicate that the entanglement attaches, and justly, some disgrace to the young Earl's name.

In Sonnet 95 the language is affectionate, but the warning is plain. A *shame*

> Doth spot the beauty of thy budding name.

The *sins* of the friend are evidently of a sexual nature, for they give rise to *lascivious comments on thy sport*, and the *dear heart* is warned that his beauty will not continue indefinitely to excuse his *vices*.

Anxiously the poet in Sonnet 96 continues his exhortations against the faults of *wantonness*, though his very *grace* may win the friend for a time forgiveness for his *faults*. The poet, in the name of his love for his friend, implores him to desist for his sake, in a couplet that exactly echoes the one in the sonnet (36) in which Shakespeare made his noble offer to sacrifice himself to shield the reputation of his friend :

> As thou being mine, mine is thy good report.

No doubt Shakespeare wished to remind his friend of a generous gesture which might well meet with some return now.

Southampton did nothing of the sort. Perhaps irritated by this reminder of the past and by the well-meant advice, he returned a hasty reply, which provoked the cold and bitter Sonnet 94. This is a strange and sarcastic piece of verse. In effect it says that the attractive who keep themselves pure are indeed the choicest of human beings, but the use of the words *stone* and *cold* gives a strangely sneering turn to the idea. The conclusion is clearer.

> Lilies that fester smell far worse than weeds.

Shakespeare, I believe, did more than merely write sonnets to Southampton during this crisis. He sat down and hastily scribbled the short poem, *A Lover's Complaint*, which he sent to his friend as a reproach, and which was long after published in the **Quarto** edition of the sonnets in 1609.

The *Complaint* is a dramatized version of the situation. Shakespeare becomes the prematurely worn maiden, deserted by her lover. The lover is Southampton to the life in feature and charm, though the golden hair is a little darkened by time. Many, like Shakespeare, got *his picture* ; many, like Shakespeare, *supposed them mistress of his heart*. He had, like Southampton, been unjustly slandered, and had been the recipient of *deep-brained sonnets*. All the gifts of others he now offers with beguiling words to his new love :

> For these, of force, must your oblations be,
> Since I their altar, you enpatron me.

He adds the ready tear to his supplications, and the damsel yields her love, only to be swiftly deserted. Yet she would fain forgive, even to be betrayed all over again.

XXVI.

REPERCUSSIONS

When Southampton received this poem, with its reproaches and accusations, its dramatized references to the past and to the present, its hint of possessive jealousy, wounded pride and perhaps a guilty conscience made him flare up in rage. Shakespeare was told in no uncertain terms to mind his own business, in which he had recently been so absorbed, and to relieve his friend of his officious advice and of his company.

The abandoned poet wrote two abject sonnets bewailing his desolation after being so harshly rejected. Terrified by the results of his rash interference, he vows in Sonnet 57 to leave his patron's business alone, and to abstain from calling him to account :

> Being your slave, what should I do but tend
> Upon the hours and times of your desire ?
> .   .   .   .
> Nor dare I question with my jealous thought
> Where you may be, or your affairs suppose.
> .   .   .   .
> So true a fool is love, that in your will
> (Though you do anything) he thinks no ill.

Sonnet 58 is equally abject, but there is an edgy note in the imploring voice :

> That God forbid that made me first your slave,
> I should in thought control your times of pleasure,

the voice moans on, but near the end a bitter sense of injustice finds expression in the glance at *self-doing crime*, and in the poignant reproach of the couplet :

> I am to wait, though waiting so be hell ;
> Not blame your pleasure, be it ill or well.

What Southampton's answer to these appeals was, it is difficult to say. As the injuring party, he may have graciously extended a qualified pardon, but the friendship was strained to breaking point. It would need only little to send it crashing in ruins. The catastrophe duly occurred.

XXVII.

A MIDSUMMER-NIGHT'S DREAM

Shakespeare, dejected by his friend's attitude, went on with his play-making. Perhaps he was completing the tragedy of the handsome weak Richard II for the Lord Chamberlain's Company.

Then a commission came his way. Lady Elizabeth Carey, god-daughter of the Queen and granddaughter of the Lord Chamberlain himself, had fallen in love with Sir Thomas Berkeley during the autumn of 1595, and the two were married at Blackfriars on 19th February, 1596. Chambers (*William Shakespeare*, Vol. I., p. 69) thinks it likely that Shakespeare was asked to write a play to celebrate the occasion. The play he wrote for this purpose was *A Midsummer-Night's Dream*.

There is an alternative theory which Chambers cites (*ibid.*) to the effect that this play was written for another wedding that took place a year previously. The evidence for this earlier dating is drawn from the topical allusions in the play. Two of the allusions are to events in 1594 ; one other :

> The thrice three Muses mourning for the death
> Of Learning, late deceas'd in beggary !

is said to refer to an event that took place more than two years before the play was composed—in September, 1592. And the person referred to is—of all people—Greene ! I cannot believe it !

I think these allusions may be read, possibly, in a different light. If the play was written at the end of 1595, then approximately a year had elapsed since the first two topical allusions mentioned above. This lapse of time is by no means a rare feature in Shakespeare's work. Harrison, in Appendix I. to his *Elizabethan Journal*, 1591–1594, quotes several examples of this time-lag. As for the third allusion, it seems to me that " sporting Kyd " is a likely candidate for the rôle. He had written other works besides plays ; he had made many translations from various foreign languages ; he was to have more than a little to do with the creation of *Hamlet* later on ; he had been disastrously associated with Marlowe and had died in abject poverty and misery just before the end of 1594. He seems to me, therefore, to be much more congenial to Shakespeare than the outrageous Greene—especially as Kyd's miserable end was the direct result of his rejection by his patron after the Marlowe association.

Now *A Midsummer-Night's Dream*, harmless and playful though it is, contained seeds of disaster for Southampton's poet. The *very tragical mirth* of the absurd Pyramus and Thisbe play, presented by the *hard-handed* workmen of Athens, was to prove tragical indeed to Shakespeare. As Chambers points out, the play was a burlesque on *Romeo and Juliet*, the play that was, I believe, specially Southampton's *own*. When the ruder sections of an audience at subsequent presentations of *Romeo and Juliet* saw that remarkable novelty on the bare Elizabethan stage, the wall over which Romeo leaps, there would be titters as the London representatives of Pyramus, Thisbe and Wall himself recalled the *man with lime and rough-cast*, the *vile wall* who represented with his fingers the *right and sinister* chink through which the lovers whispered under the moonlight. As for the death scene, it was a riot ! Pyramus thinks, erroneously, that his lady is dead, and bursts into a ludicrous parody of Romeo's passionate farewell :

> Eyes, do you see ?
> How can it be ?
> O dainty duck ! O dear !
>
> .   .   .   .   .   .
> Thus die I, thus, thus, thus.

Thisbe discovers her dead lover on the ground, and, after some brief doleful wailing, seizes his sword and perishes with these remarks :

> Come, trusty sword ;
> Come, blade, my breast imbrue :
> And farewell, friends ;—
> Thus Thisby ends ;
> Adieu, adieu, adieu.

The death scene of the incomparable lovers and Juliet's dying words :

> . . . . . O happy dagger !
> This is thy sheath ; there rust and let me die !

would be greeted with barely suppressed guffaws as the ridiculous travesty of Pyramus and Thisbe was recalled. *Romeo and Juliet* must have been ruined for the time being by this misguided piece of foolery !

Southampton, I fear, took the joke in as unappreciative a spirit as did Prince Henry the ill-timed jesting of Falstaff on the battlefield, but with less self-control. Shakespeare, in fact, got a taste of that *storm*, that *rudeness* which he had included in the description of the faithless lover of *A Lover's Complaint.*

To parody *Romeo and Juliet* was bad enough, but an even more suitable ground for a quarrel was the fact that the poet, who could not find time or inclination to write for his patron, was publicly honouring outsiders with his art. This was desertion with treachery to crown it. Southampton, irritated by the many difficulties beginning to assail him, and (who knows ?) wearied by the series of emotional crises to which his poet had subjected him, turned savagely on his friend.

XXVIII.

" A HELL OF TIME "

A note of special urgency is heard in the next group of sonnets. Shakespeare was alarmed by the new turn of events, and tried to placate his friend by protestations of devotion and apologies.

Charged with desertion and treachery, Shakespeare pleads that there was never any real unfaithfulness. Sonnet 109 opens this section :

> O, never say that I was false of heart,
> Though absence seem'd my flame to qualify.
> As easy might I from myself depart
> As from my soul, which in thy breast doth lie.

He promises amendment :

> . . . . if I have rang'd,
> Like him that travels I return again.

This last line makes it clear, I think, that the absence alluded to was purely spiritual, not physical. Shakespeare goes on to ask how it could be imagined he would

> . . . leave for nothing all thy sum of good.

Is the use of *Rose* in this sonnet a pathetic reminder of *beauty's rose* in Sonnet 1 ?

Sonnet 110 amplifies the meaning of the *stain* mentioned in Sonnet 109, in words that would well fit a reference to the foolish parody of his own fine and precious work, a parody done for the amusement of employers :

> Alas, 'tis true I have gone here and there
> And made myself a motley to the view,
> Gor'd mine own thoughts, sold cheap what is most dear ;
> Made old offences of affections new.

Having made contrite confession, the poet promises amendment with passionate fervour :

> Mine appetite I never more will grind
> On newer proof, to try an older friend.

Now all is done, in fact, and the poet asks to be reinstated in his friend's affections, never doubting he would receive a welcome. (What matter if *pure* and *loving* were slightly disingenuous descriptions now of the friend ? Things were serious, the friend was *fond on praise*, and Shakespeare was prepared to *bear all wrong*.)

The pathetically mistaken trustfulness in the friend's forgiving heart was rudely shattered by an angry repulse. Shakespeare had to reckon not only with anger but with hatred. In Sonnet 117 the poet implores pardon on any terms. " Accuse me," he says in effect, " of any crime ; say I have neglected my duty to you, say I have devoted myself to outsiders, to business, to worldly activities, but," he continues in agonized pleading,

> But shoot not at me in your waken'd hate.

Referring to the explanation offered in Sonnet 110, that the offence was committed *to try an older friend,* he urges forgiveness :

> Since my appeal says, I did strive to prove
> The constancy and virtue of your love.

The qualities of *constancy and virtue* (truth and kindness) were those for which Southampton had claimed recognition in the past. Shakespeare's excuse may be a genuine one. He had experienced a rebuff, and may have attempted in his hurt mood to re-awaken Southampton's love through jealousy. Besides, there was another factor—Elizabeth Vernon. What did these three feel about each other ? We can surmise a complex, if unacknowledged, emotional situation.

Sonnet 118 is voluble with further eager excuses and explanations why the poet tried the *bitter sauces* of new acquaintances ; because of *being full of your ne'er cloying sweetness,* he feared satiety. This, he now finds, led but to the creation of *faults assured,* instead of evading possible evils, and he assures the friend the lesson has been well learned not to attempt such folly again.

Of course all this must be a bad dream ! The friendship could not be in real danger of destruction. Crises had been met and overcome in the past by repentance and forgiveness. In Sonnet 119, self-accusation and self-blame in Hamlet fashion pour from the poet's lips. What folly ! What *wretched errors* he has committed in tampering with good through an imaginary fear that good would or could grow ill ! But all will be well :

> . . . . now I find true
> That better is by evil still made better.

Encouraged by this thought, the poet sets himself in Sonnet 120 to remind the lover of Elizabeth Vernon of a certain episode in the past, when the friend himself was in grievous error :

> That you were once unkind befriends me now.

He recalls the wrong done to him, his sufferings (*a hell of time*), feels he has not made sufficient allowances for his friend, now the victim of a similar wrong, and suffering as deeply. As tears and repentance won Shakespeare's forgiveness then, so will the friend now forgive the erring and contrite sinner :

> But that your trespass now becomes a fee ;
> Mine ransoms yours, and yours must ransom me.

As an example of innocent tactlessness, this sonnet must rank high. To bring up the Dark Lady when Southampton was in the first flush of passion for the only woman he ever loved ! To remind him of his indebtedness to the generosity of the humble player ! To recommend a similar display of magnanimous feeling on the part of the proud nobleman ! But the wisest of men could err when confused in the maelstrom of emotion, and display an almost incredible stupidity. Othello was to discover that as well as his creator.

XXIX.

" VILE ESTEEM'D " — THE END

At this point a new element intrudes into the sonnets. The poet himself, in addition to the present grief, had to endure attacks from other quarters. Unfounded slanders were attaching themselves to his name. And Southampton, incensed by the tone of Sonnet 120, had sent an angry and obdurate reply.

In Sonnet 121 Shakespeare's own anger is rising, not so much against the friend as against his traducers who are adding to his difficulties. *False adulterate eyes* spy on the poet and think they perceive looseness in his behaviour. He is *vile esteem'd* because of his alleged *sportive blood*, his *frailties*. The *frailer spies*,

> Which in their wills count bad what I think good,

are spreading rumours.

What were these rumours about ? Could it be that the ugly charge of sexual perversion had already arisen in Shakespeare's days ? Did it involve Southampton ? Shakespeare makes it clear that the accusation, whatever it was, was entirely false. He is filled with such a raging contempt that he will scarcely stoop to defend himself :

> No, I am that I am, and they that level
> At my abuses reckon up their own :
> I may be straight, though they themselves be bevel.

Sonnet 89 is a tired effort. The bid for sympathy in Sonnet 121 had failed. Now Shakespeare, in a fit of despair, gives up the attempt to defend or justify himself :

> Say that thou didst forsake me for some fault,
> And I will comment upon that offence.

He will give evidence against himself on any charge the friend likes to bring :

> For thee against myself I'll vow debate,
> For I must ne'er love him whom thou dost hate.

This piece of humility availed nothing. The reply was that the friend did hate, and Sonnet 90 seems to me a last desperate appeal from a man beset with griefs and troubles :

> Then hate me when thou wilt ; if ever, now ;
> Now, while the world is bent my deeds to cross,
> Join with the spite of fortune, make me bow,
> And do not drop in for an after-loss.
>
> .   .   .   .
>
> If thou wilt leave me, do not leave me last
> When other petty griefs have done their spite.
>
> .   .   .   .
>
> And other strains of woe, which now seem woe,
> Compar'd with loss of thee will not seem so.

And indeed the end of 1595 and the beginning of 1596 were full of troubles for Shakespeare. It may be well to summarize them at this point. On 13th September, 1595, the Lord Mayor of London was petitioning the Privy Council for the " present stay & final suppressing of . . . plays as well at the Theatre & Bankside as in all other places about the City." The reason alleged for this desired step was that play-giving fostered irreligion, " scurrilous behaviours " and riots (of which latter crime there had been several recent instances) among apprentices and other servants (Chambers, *Elizabethan Stage*, Vol. IV., p. 318). No doubt the agitation was continued for the closing of the theatres. Then, again, plague was threatening, or so it was alleged (Hotson, *Shakespeare* versus *Shallow*, p. 14). This was actually the reason given when the London theatres were later closed down on 22nd July, 1596.

Meanwhile Shakespeare's family affairs at Stratford were getting into a hopeless state of financial confusion. Both his father and his wife had borrowed money, and were in debt (Lee, *Life of Shakespeare*, p. 148). But Shakespeare's only boy Hamnet, who was dead by 11th August, 1596, must have been still alive when Sonnet 90 was penned. Not even Shakespeare's devotion to his friend could, I am sure, have led him to describe this loss *as* a *petty* grief.

But there was something more. What are we to understand by those references in Sonnet 121 to personal attacks on the poet's character ? In his fascinating book, *Shakespeare* versus *Shallow*, Dr. Leslie Hotson has come upon a curious piece of information which may find its place here and throw some light on the problem. In May and June, 1596, Francis Langley, the builder of the Swan Theatre, was expressing his opinion forcibly about a certain Gardiner : " He is a false knave ; a false forsworn knave, and a perjured knave." (*Op. cit.*, p. 26.) By November, 1596, Gardiner's stepson, William Wayte, was invoking the protection of the law against Langley and Shakespeare among others. The quarrel, already flourishing so vigorously in May, 1596, must surely have started some time earlier. Was Shakespeare involved in May ? Was he involved at an even earlier date ? Was it to this episode he refers so angrily in Sonnet 121 ? All these things seem to be not altogether outside the bounds of possibility, and the poet's language about his traducers would well fit the characters of the vile Gardiner and his utterly despicable stepson, as Dr. Hotson has shown them from contemporary records.

It was indeed a time for the poet when the world *is bent my deeds to cross*, a time of *sorrow, woe* and *petty griefs*. In Sonnet 90, in despair he had invited his friend to cast him off.

It was done. Sonnet 87 is the bitter and ironic farewell to one too good, too great for so humble a lover as the common player:

> Farewell ! thou art too dear for my possessing,
> And like enough thou know'st thy estimate :
> The charter of thy worth gives thee releasing ;
> My bonds in thee are all determinate.
> For how do I hold thee but by thy granting ?
> And for that riches where is my deserving ?
> The cause of this fair gift in me is wanting,
> And so my patent back again is swerving.
> Thyself thou gav'st, thy own worth then not knowing,
> Or me, to whom thou gav'st it, else mistaking ;
> So thy great gift, upon misprision growing,
> Comes home again, on better judgment making.
>   Thus have I had thee, as a dream doth flatter ;
>   In sleep a king, but, waking, no such matter.

AFTERMATH

I.

PICKING UP THE THREADS

In 1596—for the first time since he came to London, it is generally believed—Shakespeare revisited Stratford; and thenceforth he returned regularly to see his family. The stress of his recent experiences may be traced in the wretchedly feeble play *King John*, written according to Chambers in 1596. Harrison (*Shakespeare at Work*, p. 102) calls it " the worst thing he had written."

A request for a coat-of-arms was granted him in October, 1596. Shakespeare could not have hoped to found a family, for his only son had died just two months before. Was Shakespeare bitterly determined to become a gentleman in order that he might be subjected to no more humiliations as a common player ?

In the next year Shakespeare wrote the cynical *Henry IV* plays, with the jolly Falstaff enjoying the company of his beloved Hal, only to be rejected at the end. In these plays Chambers thinks (*William Shakespeare*, Vol. I., p. 66) that the author became " a little doubtful about the ultimate fineness of his (*i.e.*, Prince Henry's) humanity." Harrison (*Shakespeare at Work*, p. 131) describes these plays as an orgy of parodies. Real people were parodied (for instance the actor Alleyn, who had already served as Bottom in *A Midsummer-Night's Dream*) ; the characters parody themselves, " and Shakespeare parodies himself in jeering at honour." Yes, he had done this at least once before ! One wonders whether the name of Falstaff was intended as a parody on his own name, now that Greene was becoming a memory. " Shakstaff," by the way, was an alternative form of Shakespeare's name, as is recorded by Chambers (*William Shakespeare*, Vol. II., p. 372).

As for Southampton, he found it advisable to quit the Court, and tried to join the Earl of Essex, who was planning his great attack on Cadiz. Southampton was unsuccessful, and retired to brood over his troubles at his country home of Titchfield (Mrs. Stopes, *Life*, Ch. VIII.). He is not recorded as being at Court at any time during 1596. Nor at this period did he make any attempt to be married to Elizabeth Vernon.

II.

A LETTER FROM THE COUNTESS OF SOUTHAMPTON

A curious letter from the Countess of Southampton—for the Earl did eventually wed his Elizabeth Vernon under romantic and dangerous circumstances in 1598—has been preserved. It is dated 8th July (1599) and was sent to him to Ireland, where he was campaigning after his brief spell in the Tower. It runs as follows :

> All the news I can send you that I think will make you merry is that I read in a letter from London that Sir John Falstaff is by hîs Mistress Dame Pintpot made father of a goodly miller's thumb, a boy that's all head and very little body ; but this is a secret.

Chambers doubts if the reference is to Shakespeare (*William Shakespeare*, Vol. II., p. 198). So does Mrs. Stopes (*Life of Southampton*, p. 160). Neither offers any satisfactory alternative explanation of the allusion. " Pintpot " is of course Falstaff's jesting name for the hostess of the Boar's Head Tavern (*Henry IV.*, *Part I.*, II. iv.). Was it also a name for the Dark Lady ? Did Shakespeare return to her after he had lost Southampton ? Did he write sonnets to her again, and were these the " certain other sonnets by W.S." included in " *Amours* by J.D.," entered in the Stationers' Register on 3rd January, 1600 ? The book was promptly suppressed (Robertson, p. 121). A return to the Dark Lady would at any rate explain the wonderful character of Cleopatra.

As for the " Falstaff " allusion there is some evidence which may suggest that Shakespeare was known in jest by the name of his most popular character. In the " Collection of letters made by Sir Tobie Matthews, Kt. 1660 " (quoted in *The Shakspere Allusion Book*, Vol. I., p. 88) occurs this passage :

> " (as that excellent author, Sir John Falstaff, says) what for your business, news, device, foolery and liberty, I never dealt better since I was a man."

These last words are indeed spoken by Falstaff (*Henry IV., Part I.,* II. iv.) ; but the use of the term *author* might suggest that the writer was actually thinking of Shakespeare himself.

It is very likely that the Countess would send any bit of gossip she could pick up about his old friend to the Earl, and there is a very human touch of feminine spite about the telling of this rather shabby little anecdote.

III.

THE YEAR 1603

In 1603 Southampton, after lying in the Tower, a prisoner convicted of high treason and under sentence of death for his share in the Essex rising, was released by the new king, James I. In 1603–4, Chambers thinks (*William Shakespeare*, Vol. I., p. 271), Shakespeare wrote no plays.

IV.

PUBLICATION OF THE SONNETS

Mary, the fair mother of the Earl of Southampton, was married in 1598 to her old friend Mr. (now Sir) William Harvey. She died in 1607, and in the next year Harvey was married again. On 20th May, 1609, the book *Shakespeare's Sonnets* was entered in the Stationers' Register, and published with the famous dedication to " Mr. W.H.," the " only begetter " of the sonnets.

Sir William Harvey is now widely accepted as the solution to the problem of identifying Mr. W.H., and I need not here recapitulate the very convincing arguments in his favour. It seems likely that the printer Thorpe knew nothing of the circumstances surrounding the writing of the sequence. He may have been told that Harvey originally suggested the writing of the sonnets, and this would account for the wording of the dedication. But Harvey had just been married, and T.T. may have blundered into the error of thinking that the early marriage sonnets (as well as the rest of the poetry) had been addressed to Harvey himself. If this were the case, the intention of the dedication becomes even clearer. These surmises have all been considered at various times by students of the sonnets.

What follow are a few speculations of my own. I imagine that the Dark Lady sonnets were found with the series to Southampton, but in a separate packet, and hence they were placed in a group at the end of the larger sequence. Shakespeare's poor little effort, *A Lover's Complaint*, was also found at the same time where it had been placed with the other verses. The whole bundle was handed over to Thorpe for printing and publication, and he arranged the poems simply in the order in which they had come into his hands.

Various reasons, such as the poor quality of the paper on which the sonnets are printed and the number of misprints, have suggested to critics that Shakespeare did not have anything to do with the publication, and indeed may have been unaware of what was going on. The method of setting forth the titles in the Quarto, too, is odd. The poem is described as *A Louers complaint. | by | William Shake-speare.* The sonnets are entitled *Shake-speares, | sonnets.*, as if the printer thought the author's name part of the title. This, however, is a minor point. Shakespeare in 1609 was a wealthy man, who could have afforded to give his sonnets a more worthy setting, had he wished to do so. But would he, even at that late date, or would Southampton, have consented to the appearance in print of such intimate revelations ? It has been suggested that the issue was soon suppressed, as only some dozen copies seem to have survived to-day. Was Shakespeare or Southampton instrumental in this matter ? During the lifetime of both men there was no further issue.

Why were the sonnets printed in the first place ? We can only guess, and this is my guess. If Harvey was the agent the publication may have been intended as a spiteful shot at his haughty ex-stepson, Southampton. There had been bad feeling between mother and son over her marriage with a comparative commoner such as Harvey. Apparently, too, before the marriage Harvey had assumed a truculent attitude towards the young man on account of his openly expressed objections, and Essex was called in to make peace. Harvey's insolence took the form of

saying that if the young Earl did not like the marriage, he would
—in modern slang phrase—have to lump it. " They that were
angry without cause, must be pleased without amends," are his
own words as reported by Essex in a letter to Southampton in
November, 1597 (Mrs. Stopes, *Life of Southampton*, p. 135). This
business was bound to rankle on both sides. Once the mother
was dead, Harvey needed no longer to conceal his feelings. He
may have come across the bundles of poems in a drawer during
the household upheaval after the death of his wife, and seen in
them a pretty method of revenge on his supercilious stepson.
Their publication would give pain to Southampton. And it could
be shown that he too, for all his haughty airs, had in his time
not only consorted with, but made a bosom friend of a commoner
fellow than Harvey. To his petty malice, perhaps, we owe a
deep debt of gratitude.

V.

THE LAST PLAYS

What did Shakespeare think when the sonnets appeared ?
There is no record of his reactions, unless we look for them in
his later plays. From 1609 till he ceased play-writing (if we
except the dubious *Henry VIII.* and *The Two Noble Kinsmen*),
Shakespeare was creating a new kind of play—the play of forgiveness. Wrongs inflicted and endured, partings, and, after the
passing of time, final pardon though the scars remain : these are
the themes of *The Winter's Tale* (did Shakespeare remember the
fatal *A Midsummer-Night's Dream* when he chose the title of
this play with its silently forgiving Hermione ?), *Cymbeline* and
The Tempest. And the themes had already been adumbrated in
the sonnets themselves. We may make what we please of this
final phrase. " The rest is silence."

VI.

PUBLICATION OF THE FOLIO

In 1623 the first Folio of Shakespeare's works appeared with
a dedication to William Herbert, Earl of Pembroke. Chambers
(*William Shakespeare*, Vol. I., p. 567) mentions this as support

for the theory to which he inclines—that the friend of the sonnets was Herbert and not Southampton. It may be argued with equal justice that the dedication indicates the exact opposite. The sonnets, I believe, show that the breach between the friends was bitter and final in its character. It would have been strange indeed if under these circumstances Southampton had accepted, or even been approached to accept the dedication. Nor can we imagine Shakespeare would have wished to place his plays, the cause of all the trouble, under the patronage of the man who had so decisively rejected him. Heminge and Condell, Shakespeare's friends and remembered in his will, may not have known the story ; on the other hand Shakespeare may have told them something of it, and then it would have been a clumsy, tactless blunder to try to force the dedication on Southampton.

LIST OF PRINCIPAL BOOKS CONSULTED.

CHAMBERS, E. K. *The Elizabethan Stage*, 4 vols. 1923.

CHAMBERS, E. K. *William Shakespeare : A Study of Facts and Problems*, 2 vols. 1930.

GREENE, R. *Groats-worth of Witte*. The Bodley Head Quartos. 1923.

HARRISON, G. B. *An Elizabethan Journal* . . . 1591–1594. 1928.

HARRISON, G. B. *Shakespeare at Work*, 1592–1603. 1933.

HOTSON, L. *Shakespeare* versus *Shallow*. 1931.

HUME, M. A. S. *Sir Walter Ralegh*. 1906.

JUSSERAND, J. J. *The English Novel in the Time of Shakespeare*. 1901.

LEE, S. *A Life of William Shakespeare*. 1899.

LEE, S. (ed.) *Elizabethan Sonnets*, Vol. I. 1904.

NEALE, J. E. *Queen Elizabeth*. 1934.

ROBERTSON, J. M. *The Problems of the Shakespeare Sonnets*. 1926.

SHAKESPEARE'S SONNETS. *A Facsimile of the Quarto Edition*. Jonathan Cape. 1925.

STOPES, C. C. *The Life of Henry, Third Earl of Southampton, Shakespeare's Patron*. 1922.

STRICKLAND, A. *The Life of Queen Elizabeth*. 1915.

THE SHAKSPERE ALLUSION BOOK, 2 vols. 1909.

THOMSON, W. *The Sonnets of Shakespeare and Southampton*. 1938.

THORNDIKE, R. *A Wanderer with Shakespeare*. 1940.

TUCKER, T. G. (ed.) *The Sonnets of Shakespeare*. 1924.

INDEX

(Reference to particular sonnets will be found on the pages indicated.)

200.

5

18   29   54   18   33
      71   129   33   64
           146   144   73
                     121   76
                               144

9
30
64
54
55
106